YOU CAN TEACH YOURSELF ®

FOLK SINGING GUITAR

By Jerry Silverman

Contents—Section One

Lesson 1
How To Hold The Guitar

The six open strings of the guitar are numbered in consecutive order from the first (the thinnest — the one with the highest pitch) to the sixth (the thickest — the one with the lowest pitch).

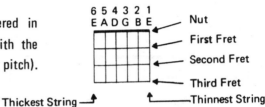

You will notice that in addition to the numbers, the strings also have letter (that is, note) names. The six open strings of the guitar are written as follows:

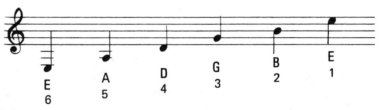

The fingers of the left hand are numbered as follows:

Index finger = 1
Middle finger = 2
Ring finger = 3
Pinky = 4

These are the fingers which are generally used in playing chords. The thumb is used for support — pressing against the back of the neck of the guitar. To play a chord properly you must first of all have very short fingernails on your left hand. This is so because you must press straight down on the strings hard enough to bring them into firm contact with the *frets* (the metal strips under the strings). Place your fingers close to the frets (as shown in the diagrams). Be careful not to muffle any neighboring string with the side of a finger or with your palm.

Key of D

D CHORD

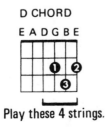

Play these 4 strings.

Place fingers close to frets.

A7 CHORD

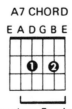

Play these 5 strings.

BASIC THUMB—STRUM IN $\frac{2}{4}$

Play each chord four times, strumming downward with your thumb. Play only the strings indicated in the diagram. Practice switching back and forth between D and A7.

Before you start to sing always play the first chord of the song in the rhythm of the song. This should help give you the pitch of the first note.

So . . . strum D slowly . . . Follow the vertical slashes for the rhythm.

Skip To My Lou

D
Lost my partner, what'll I do?
A7
Lost my partner, what'll I do?
D
Lost my partner, what'll I do?
A7   **D**
Skip to my Lou, my darling. *Chorus*

D
Little red wagon painted blue,
A7
Little red wagon painted blue,
D
Little red wagon painted blue,
A7   **D**
Skip to my Lou, my darling. *Chorus*

D
I'll get another one prettier than you,
A7
I'll get another one prettier than you,
D
I'll get another one prettier than you,
A7   **D**
Skip to my Lou, my darling. *Chorus*

D
Flies in the buttermilk, shoo fly, shoo,
A7
Flies in the buttermilk, shoo fly, shoo,
D
Flies in the buttermilk, shoo fly, shoo,
A7   **D**
Skip to my Lou, my darling. *Chorus*

D
Gone again, skip to my Lou,
A7
Gone again, skip to my Lou,
D
Gone again, skip to my Lou,
A7   **D**
Skip to my Lou, my darling. *Chorus*

G CHORD

The Thumb—Finger Pluck

From now on the thumb will no longer be the only finger used in striking the chords. The thumb is now assigned to the proper bass note (depending on the chord) and the three fingers now pluck the first three strings as follows:

Finger a G chord.

Rest the thumb on the sixth string and bring the tips of the fingers one, two and three into contact lightly with strings three, two and one, respectively.

Thumb strikes sixth string . . . followed by . . . the three fingers plucking upward together on the first three strings.

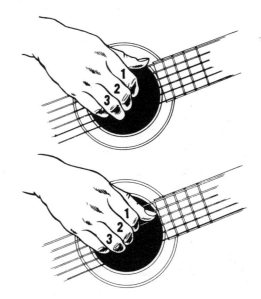

Try the same pattern with a D chord (thumb on fourth string) and an A7 (thumb on fifth string).

Goin' Across The Mountain

Goin' a - cross the moun - tain Oh, fare you well,

Goin' a - cross the moun - tain, You can hear my ban - jo tell.

D	D	D
Got my rations on my back	Goin' across the mountain	I expect you'll miss me when I'm gone
A7	**A7**	**A7**
My powder it is dry	If I have to crawl	But I'm goin' through
D	**D**	**D**
I'm a-goin' across the mountain	To give old Jeff's men	When this war is over
G **D**	**G** **D**	**G** **D**
Chrissie, don't you cry.	A little of my rifle ball.	I'll come back to you.

D	D	D
Goin' across the mountain	Way before it's good daylight	Goin' across the mountain
A7	**A7**	**A7**
To join the boys in Blue	If nothing happens to me	Oh, fare you well
D	**D**	**D**
When this war is over	I'll be way down yonder	Goin' across the mountain
G **D**	**G** **D**	**G** **D**
I'll come back to you.	In old Tennessee.	Oh, fare you well.

Roll On The Ground

Based on a traditional song.
Additional Lyrics by
JERRY SILVERMAN

Chorus

Roll on the ground, boys, Roll on the ground, Eat so - da

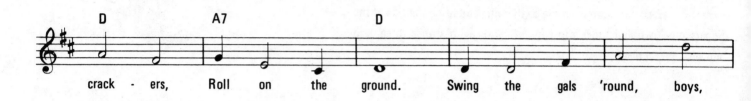

crack - ers, Roll on the ground. Swing the gals 'round, boys,

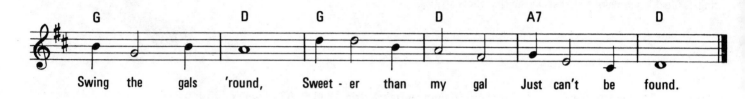

Swing the gals 'round, Sweet - er than my gal Just can't be found.

D Work on the railroad,	**D** Big ball's in Nashville,
G **D** Dollar a day.	**G** **D** Big ball's in town.
G **D** Eat soda crackers,	**G** **D** Eat soda crackers,
A7 **D** Wind blow'em away.	**A7** **D** Roll on the ground.
Wind blow'em away, boys,	Roll on the ground, boys,
G **D** Wind blow'em away.	**G** **D** Roll on the ground.
G **D** Eat soda crackers,	**G** **D** Eat soda crackers,
A7 **D** Wind blow'em away. *Chorus*	**A7** **D** Roll on the ground. *Chorus*

D
Goin' up to Nashville,
G   **D**
Have me a time.
G   **D**
Eat soda crackers,
A7   **D**
Ten for a dime.

Ten for a dime, boys,
G   **D**
Ten for a dime.
G   **D**
Eat soda crackers,
A7   **D**
Ten for a dime. *Chorus*

My Home's Across The Smoky Mountains

Based on a traditional song.
Additional Lyrics by
JERRY SILVERMAN

My home's a - cross the Smok - y Moun - tains, My
home's a - cross the Smok - y Moun - tains, My
home's a - cross the Smok - y Moun - tains, And I'll
nev - er get to see you an - y - more, more, more; ___ And I'll
nev - er get to see you an - y - more. ___

D
Goodbye, honey, sugar darling.
A7   **D**
Goodbye, honey, sugar darling.

Goodbye, honey, sugar darling,
    G   **A7**   **D**
And I'll never get to see you anymore, more, more;
    G   **A7**   **D**
I'll never get to see you anymore.

D
I'm bound to cross that lonesome valley.
A7   **D**
I'm bound to cross that lonesome valley.

I'm bound to cross that lonesome valley,
    G   **A7**   **D**
And I'll never get to see you anymore, more, more;
    G   **A7**   **D**
I'll never get to see you anymore.

                    D
So, don't you grieve for me, my darling.
    A7   **D**
Don't you grieve for me, my darling.

Don't you grieve for me, my darling.
    G   **A7**   **D**
And I'll never get to see you anymore, more, more;
    G   **A7**   **D**
I'll never get to see you anymore.

Cripple Creek

I got a gal at the head of the creek,

Go up and see her 'bout the mid-dle of the week.

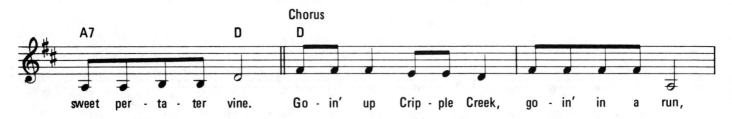

Kiss her on the mouth, just as sweet as an-y wine, Wraps her-self a-round me like a

Chorus

sweet per-ta-ter vine. Go-in' up Crip-ple Creek, go-in' in a run,

Go-in' up Crip-ple Creek to have a lit-tle fun. Go-in' up Crip-ple Creek,

go-in' in a whirl, Go-in' up Crip-ple Creek to see my girl.

	D		G	D

D   G   D
Girls on the Cripple Creek 'bout half grown,
            A7   D
Jump on a boy like a dog on a bone.
            G   D
Roll my britches above my knees,
            A7   D
Wade old Cripple Creek when I please. *Chorus*

D   G   D
Cripple Creek's wide and Cripple Creek's deep,
               A7   D
I'll wade old Cripple Creek afore I sleep.
               G   D
Roads are rocky and the hillside's muddy,
              A7   D
And I'm so drunk that I can't stand steady. *Chorus*

The Bold Soldier

Soldier, oh soldier, a comin' from the plain. Court-ed a lady through hon-or and through fame. Her beau-ty shone so bright that it nev-er could be told. She al-ways loved the sol-dier be-cause he was so bold. Fa-la-la-la, ____ ____ Fa-la-la-la-la, ____ Fa-la-la-la, ____ Fa-la-la-la. ____

D   A7
Soldier, O soldier, it's I would be thy bride,
D   A7   D
But for fear of my father some danger might betide.

                                  A7
Then he pulled out sword and pistol and he hung 'em by his side,
D   A7   D
Swore he would be married, no matter what betide. *Chorus*

         D   A7
Then he took her to the parson, and, of course, home again;
         D   A7   D
There they met her father and seven armed men.

                             A7
"Let us fly, " said the lady, "I fear we shall be slain."
             D   A7   D
"Hold your hand," said the soldier, "Never fear again." *Chorus*

         D   A7
Then he pulled out sword and pistol and he caused them to rattle;
         D   A7   D
The lady held the horse while the soldier fought in battle.

                           A7
"Hold your hand," said the old man, "do not be so bold;
         D   A7   D
You shall have my daughter and a thousand pounds of gold." *Chorus*

         D   A7
"Fight on!" said the lady, "the portion is too small."
             D   A7   D
"Hold your hand," said the old man, "you can have it all."

                                    A7
Then he took them right straight home and he called them son and dear,
         D   A7   D
Not because he loved them but only through fear. *Chorus*

Deadheads and Suckers

D
I'm goin' around the mountain,

Bound to leave you now,
G
Bound to leave you now, darlin'
D
Bound to leave you now.

Goin' around the mountain,

Bound to leave you now,
A7   **D**
And darlin', I don't know what to do. *Chorus*

D
Light in the graveyard,

It outshines the sun,
G
It outshines the sun, darlin',
D
It outshines the sun.

Light in the graveyard,

It outshines the sun,
A7   **D**
And darlin', I don't know what to do. *Chorus*

D
High Sheriff and the police

Runnin' after me,
G
Runnin' after me, darlin',
D
Runnin' after me.

High Sheriff and the police

Runnin' after me,
A7   **D**
And Lordy, I don't know what to do. *Chorus*

D
Mighty happy meeting,

Don't you want to go?
G
Don't you want to go, darlin',
D
Don't you want to go?

Mighty happy meeting,

Don't you want to go,
A7   **D**
Way over on the other shore? *Chorus*

Oleanna

Based on a traditional melody
Lyrics by
JERRY SILVERMAN

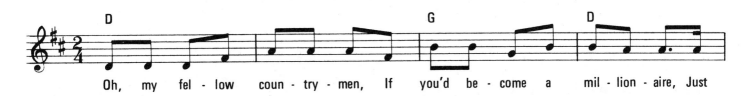

Oh, my fel - low coun - try - men, If you'd be - come a mil - lion - aire, Just

head for O - le - an - na, All your fond - est dreams will come true there,

Chorus

O - le, O - le - an - na, O - le, O - le - an - na,

O - le, O - le, O - le, O - le, O - le, O - le - an - na.

D
Anywhere you take a walk,
G   **D**
And this is true, so I've been told,
A7   **D**
If you chance to stub your toe,
       A7   **D**
'Twill be against a lump of gold. *Chorus*

D
When it's time to go to work,
G   **D**
And here you'll have a big surprise;
A7   **D**
No sooner do you reach your job,
A7   **D**
Than they close for holidays. *Chorus*

D
Talk about good things to eat,
G   **D**
They've got them there, and that's no lie.
A7   **D**
Apple strudle, apple dumplings,
A7   **D**
Apple-sauce and apple pie. *Chorus*

D
Oleanna, that's the place,
G   **D**
That's the place for you and me,
A7   **D**
Where they pay you to relax.
       A7   **D,**
And when you sleep, it's double fee. *Chorus*

Lesson 2
Key of A

A CHORD   E7 CHORD

THE THUMB—FINGER PLUCK IN $\frac{3}{4}$

The accompaniment for a song in three-quarter time is quite simple. It is merely an extension of the basic thumb-finger pluck into a thumb-finger-finger pluck.

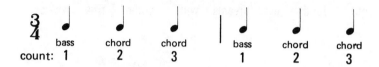

For the A chord the thumb strikes the A (5th) string. Let's try a nice easy going three-quarter time strum on A . . .

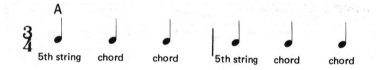

For the E7 chord the thumb strikes the E (6th) string. Now try the strum on E7 . . . Then practice switching from A to E7. When you feel you can do it comfortably try it with a D chord. The D chord is commonly found in the key of A.

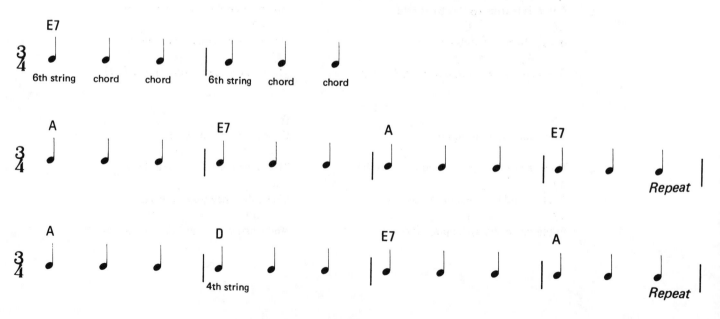

Rye Whiskey

Rye whis-key, rye whis-key, rye whis-key, I cry. If I

don't get rye whis-key, I sure-ly will die.

A
It's whiskey, rye whiskey,

I know you of old,

You robbed my poor pockets
E7   A
Of silver and gold. *Chorus*

A
It's beefsteak when I'm hungry,

Rye whiskey when I'm dry,

A greenback when I'm hard up,
E7   A
Oh, Heaven when I die. *Chorus*

A
I go to yonder holler

And I'll build me a still,

And I'll give you a gallon
E7   A
For a five-dollar bill. *Chorus*

A
If the ocean was whiskey

And I was duck,

I'd dive to the bottom
E7   A
And never come up. *Chorus*

A
But the ocean ain't whiskey

And I ain't a duck.

So I'll play Jack o' Diamonds
E7   A
And trust to my luck. *Chorus*

A
Her parents don't like me,

They say I'm too poor,

And I'm unfit
E7   A
To darken her door. *Chorus*

A
Her parents don't like me,

Well, my money's my own,

And them that don't like me
E7   A
Can leave me alone. *Chorus*

A
Oh whiskey, you villain,

You're no friend to me,

You killed my poor pappy,
E7   A
God-damn you, try me. *Chorus*

Springfield Mountain

On Spring-field Moun - tain, there did dwell A love - ly youth I knew him well.____

Chorus

Too roo di noo, too roo di nay, Too roo di noo, too roo di nay.

A E7 This lovely youth one day did go A Down to the meadow for to mow. *Chorus*	A E7 This took him home to Molly dear, A Which made him feel so very queer. *Chorus*
A E7 He had not mowed quite round the field A When a p'izen sarpent bit his heel. *Chorus*	A E7 Now Molly had two ruby lips A With which the p'izen she did sip. *Chorus*

A   E7
Now Molly had a rotting tooth
A
And so the p'izen killed them both. *Chorus*

ALTERNATING BASS NOTES

The thumb does not always have to strike one string per chord. In fact, a very pleasing musical effect is obtained if the thumb alternates between certain specific strings, depending on what chord is being played.

The alternate bass notes for the chords we have learned are as follows:

A	6th string (also 4th)
E7	5th string
D	5th string
G	5th string (also 4th)
A7	6th and 4th strings

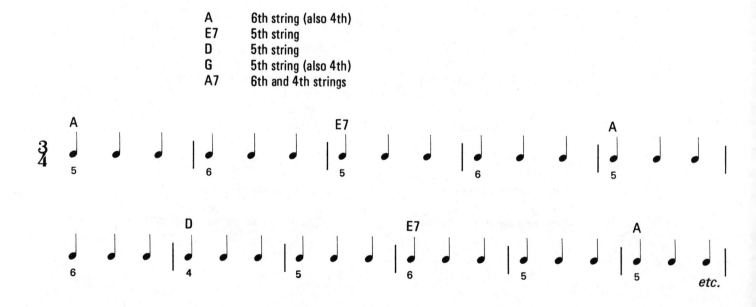

I Ride An Old Paint

I ride an old paint,— I lead an old dan,— I'm goin' to Mon-

tan - a to throw the Hou - li - han, They feed in the cou - lees, they

wa - ter in the draw, Their tails are all mat - ted, their backs are all raw.

Chorus

Ride a - round, lit - tle do - gies, ride a - round____ them____

slow, For the fier - y and snuf - fy are rar - in' to go.

A
Old Bill Jones had two daughters and a song,
E7   A
One went to college the other went wrong.
E7   A
His wife got killed in a pool-room fight,
E7   A
But still he keeps singing from morning till night. *Chorus*

A
I've worked in the city, worked on the farm,
E7   A
And all I've got to show is the muscle in my arm.
E7   A
Patches on my pants, callous on my hand
E7   A
And I'm goin' to Montana to throw the houlihan. *Chorus*

A
When I die, don't bury me at all,
E7   A
Put me on my pony and lead him from his stall.
E7   A
Tie my bones to his back, turn our faces to the west,
E7   A
And we'll ride the prairie that we love the best. *Chorus*

Revolutionary Tea

There was an old la - dy lived o - ver the sea, And she was an
old la - dy's pock - ets were filled up with gold, But nev - er con -

is ____ land queen. ____ Her daugh - ter lived off in a new ____ coun -
tent - ed, she. ____ She called on her daugh - ter to pay ____ to

1.
try, With an o - cean of wa - ter be - tween. ____ The
her, Tax of three pence a pound on her

2.
tea, of three pence a pound on her tea. ____

A   E7
"Now mother, dear mother," the daughter replied,
A   D   E7
"I sha'n't do the thing that you ax.
A   E7
I'm willing to pay a fair price for the tea,
A   E7   A
But never a threepenny tax."

  E7
"You shall!" quoth the mother, and reddened with rage,
A   D   E7
"For you're my own daughter, you see.
A   E7
And sure, 'tis quite proper the daughter should pay
A   E7   A
Her mother a tax on the tea,
D   A   E7   A
Her mother a tax on the tea."

A   E7
And so the old lady her servant called up,
A   D   E7
And packed off a budget of tea.
A   E7
And eager for three pence a pound, she put in
A   E7   A
Enough for a large family.

  E7
She ordered her servant to bring home the tax,
A   D   E7
Declaring her child should obey,
A   E7
Or old as she was and a woman most grown,
A   E7   A
She'd half whip her life away,
D   A   E7   A
She'd half whip her life away.

A   E7
The tea was conveyed to the daughter's door
A   D   E7
All down by the oceanside.
A   E7
But the bouncing girl poured out every last pound
A   E7   A
In the dark and the boiling tide.

  E7
And then she called out to the Island Queen,
A   D   E7
"Oh mother, dear mother," quoth she,
A   E7
"Your tea you may have when it is steeped enough,
A   E7   A
But never a tax from me,
D   A   E7   A
But never a tax from me."

1-15

Billy The Kid

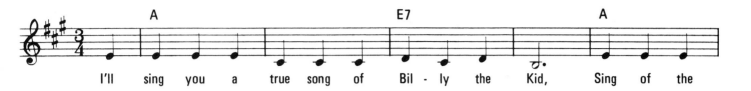

I'll sing you a true song of Bil - ly the Kid, Sing of the

des - per - ate deeds that he did, Way out in New Mex - i - co

long, long a - go Where a man's on - ly friend was his old for - ty - four.

A   E7
When Billy the Kid was a very young lad,
A   E7
In old Silver City he went to the bad.
A   D
Way out in the West with a gun in his hand,
E7   A
At the age of twelve years he killed his first man.

A   E7
Young Mexican maidens play guitars and sing
A   E7
Songs about Billy, their boy bandit king,
A   D
How there's a young man who had reached his sad end—
E7   A
Had a notch on his pistol for twenty-one men.

A   E7
It was on the same night when poor Billy died,
A   E7
He said to his friends, "I'm not satisfied.
A   D
There are twenty-one men I have put bullets through
E7   A
Sheriff Pat Garritt must make twenty-two."

A   E7
Now this is how Billy the Kid met his fate,
A   E7
The bright moon was shining, the hour was late.
A   D
Shot down by Pat Garritt who once was his friend,
E7   A
The young outlaw's life had now reached its sad end.

A   E7
Now there's many a lad with a face fine and fair,
A   E7
Who starts out in life with a chance to be square,
A   D
But just like poor Billy they wander astray,
E7   A
They lose their life in the very same way.

The Devil and The Farmer's Wife

The Dev-il come up to the farm-er one day, Tee-roo, tee-roo, to the farm-er one day, Says, "One of your fam-'ly I'm tak-ing a-way, Tee-roo, tee-roo, I'm tak-ing a-way."

A
"Oh, please don't take my eldest son,
D   **A**
"Teeroo, teeroo, my eldest son,

                   E7
"There's work on the farm that's got to be done,
               A
"Teeroo, teeroo, that's got to be done.

*The 2nd and 4th lines of each verse begin with
"teeroo, teeroo" and end with the last few
words of their respective verses, as above.

"Take my wife, take my wife with the joy of my heart. . .
"And I hope, by golly, that you never part. . .

The Devil put the old lady into a sack. . .
And down the road he goes clickety-clack. . .

When the Devil got her to the fork in the road. . .
He says, "Old woman, you're a hell of a load. . .

When the Devil got her to the gates of hell. . .
He says, "Poke up the fires, we'll bake her well. . .

Up came a little devil with a ball and chain. . .
She upped with her foot and she kicked out his brains. . .

Then nine little devils went climbing the wall. . .
Screaming, "Take her back, Daddy, she'll murder us all. . .

The old man was peeping out of the shack. . .
When he saw the old Devil come bringing her back. . .

He says, "Here's your wife, both sound and well. . .
"If I kept her there longer she'd have torn up hell. . .

He says, "I've been a devil most all of my life. . .
"But I've never been in hell till I met with your wife. . .

This proves that the women are better than men. . .
They can all go to hell and come back again. . .

Sweet Betsy From Pike

A   E7   A
One evening quite early they camped on the Platte,
E7
'Twas near by the road on a green shady flat;
A   D   A
Where Betsy, quite tired, lay down to repose,
E7   A
While with wonder, Ike gazed on his Pike County rose. *Chorus*

A   E7   A
The Shanghai ran off and their cattle all died,
E7
That morning the last piece of bacon was fried.
A   D   A
Poor Ike got discouraged and Betsy got mad,
E7   A
The dog drooped his tail and looked wondrously sad. *Chorus*

A   E7   A
They soon reached the desert where Betsy gave out,
E7
And down in the sand she lay rolling about.
A   D   A
While Ike in great terror looked on in surprise,
E7   A
Saying, "Betsy, get up, you'll get sand in your eyes." *Chorus*

A   E7   A
They swam the wide rivers and crossed the tall peaks,
E7
They camped on the prairie for weeks upon weeks.
A   D   A
Starvation and cholera, hard work and slaughter,
E7   A
They reached California spite of hell and high water. *Chorus*

A   E7   A
Long Ike and Sweet Betsy attended a dance,
E7
And Ike wore a pair of his Pike County pants.
A   D   A
Sweet Betsy was dressed up in ribbons and rings,
E7   A
Says Ike, "You're an angel, but where are your wings?" *Chorus*

A   E7   A
A miner said, "Betsy, will you dance with me?"
E7
"I will, you old hoss, if you don't make too free.
A   D   A
But don't dance me hard—do you want to know why?
E7   A
Doggone ye, I'm chock-full of strong alkali!" *Chorus*

A   E7   A
Long Ike and Sweet Betsy got married, of course,
E7
But Ike getting jealous, obtained a divorce.
A   D   A
And Betsy, well satisfied, said with a shout,
E7   A
"Goodbye, you big lummox, I'm glad you backed out!" *Chorus*

D# dim. (D#°)

The Bowery

Words by
CHARLES H. HOYT

Music by
PERCY GAUNT

Oh! the night that I struck New York I went out for a qui-et
But I went to en-joy the sights, There was the Bow-'ry a-blaze with

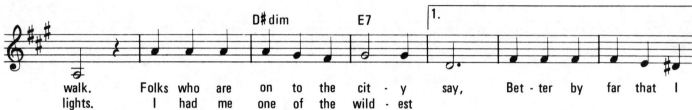

walk. Folks who are on to the cit-y say, Bet-ter by far that I
lights. I had me one of the wild-est

took Broad-way. nights. I'll nev-er go there an-y-more.

Chorus

The Bow-'ry, The Bow-'ry! They say such things and they do strange

things on the Bow-'ry, The Bow-'ry! I'll nev-er go there an-y-more.

A	E7
I had walked but a block or two,
A
When up came a fellow and me he knew.
D# dim   E7
Then a policeman came walking by,
A
Chased him away, and I asked him why.
E7
"Wasn't he pulling your leg?" said he.
A
Said I, "He never laid hands on me!"
D# dim   E7
"Get off the Bowery, you fool!" said he.
A
I'll never go there any more. *Chorus*

A   E7
Struck a place that they called a "dive,"
A
I was in luck to get out alive.
D# dim   E7
When the policeman, he heard my woes,
A
Saw my black eyes and my battered nose,
E7
"You've been held up!" then the copper said.
A
"No, sir! but I've been knocked down instead."
D# dim   E7
Then he just laughed, though I couldn't see why.
A
I'll never go there any more. *Chorus*

Lesson 3
Key of G

G CHORD

C CHORD

D7 CHORD

BASIC ARPEGGIO IN $\frac{4}{4}$

The fingers of the right hand may pluck the strings one at a time in various patterns and combinations. Chords played in this manner are called *arpeggios*.

First, finger a G chord and move the fingers of the right hand as follows:

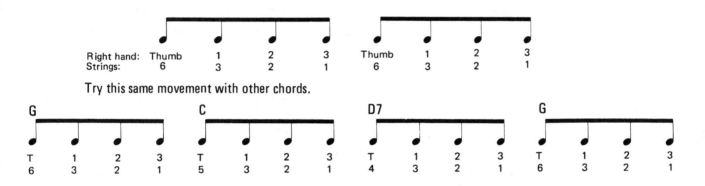

Right hand: Thumb 1 2 3 Thumb 1 2 3
Strings: 6 3 2 1 6 3 2 1

Try this same movement with other chords.

Now we will add two quarter notes — the usual bass-chord strum *before* the four eighth notes of the arpeggio. Be sure to time the whole sequence correctly so that the "one-two" of the bass-chord strum and the "three-and-four-and" of the arpeggio are equal in total playing time.

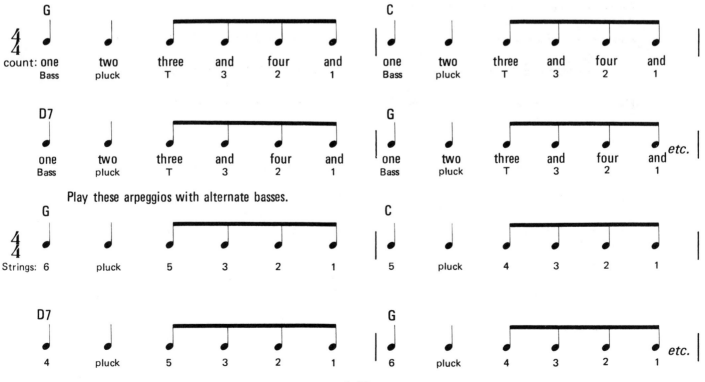

Mama Don't 'Low

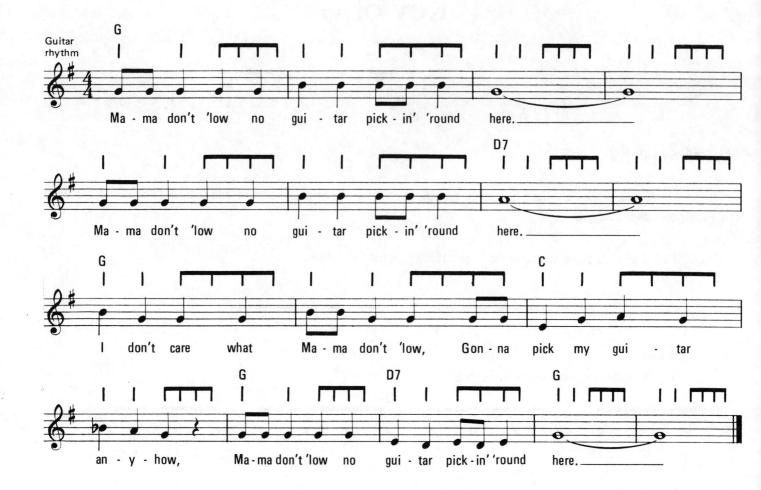

Ma - ma don't 'low no gui - tar pick - in' 'round here.

Ma - ma don't 'low no gui - tar pick - in' 'round here.

I don't care what Ma - ma don't 'low, Gon - na pick my gui - tar

an - y - how, Ma - ma don't 'low no gui - tar pick - in' 'round here.

G
Mama don't 'low no banjo playin' 'round here,
D7
Mama don't 'low no banjo playin' 'round here,
G
I don't care what mama don't 'low,
C
Gonna play my banjo anyhow.
G   D7   G
Mama don't 'low no banjo playin' 'round here.

G
Mama don't 'low no cigar smokin' 'round here,
D7
Mama don't 'low no cigar smokin' 'round here,
G
I don't care what mama don't 'low,
C
Gonna smoke my cigar anyhow.
G   D7   G
Mama don't 'low no cigar smokin' 'round here.

G
Mama don't 'low no midnight ramblin' 'round here,
D7
Mama don't 'low no midnight ramblin' 'round here,
G
I don't care what mama don't 'low,
C
Gonna ramble midnights anyhow.
G   D7   G
Mama don't 'low no midnight ramblin' 'round here.

G
Mama don't 'low no whiskey drinkin' 'round here,
D7
Mama don't 'low no whiskey drinkin' 'round here,
G
I don't care what mama don't 'low,
C
Gonna drink my whiskey anyhow.
G   D7   G
Mama don't 'low no whiskey drinkin' 'round here.

Worried Man Blues

Guitar rhythm

G

It takes a wor-ried man to sing a wor-ried song, It

continue strum

C

takes a wor-ried man to sing a wor-ried song, It takes a wor-ried man to

G

D7

sing a wor-ried song, I'm wor-ried now _____ but I won't be wor-ried long.

G

G
I went across the river and I lay down to sleep,
C   G
I went across the river and I lay down to sleep,

I went across the river and I lay down to sleep,
       D7   G
When I woke up — had shackles on my feet. *Chorus*

G
Twenty-nine links of chain around my leg,
C   G
Twenty-nine links of chain around my leg,

Twenty-nine links of chain around my leg,
       D7   G
And on each link, an initial of my name. *Chorus*

G
I asked the judge, "What's gonna be my fine?"
C   G
I asked the judge, "What's gonna be my fine?"

I asked the judge, "What's gonna be my fine?"
       D7   G
"Twenty-one years on the Rocky Mountain Line." *Chorus*

G
Twenty-one years to pay my awful crime,
C   G
Twenty-one years to pay my awful crime,

Twenty-one years to pay my awful crime,
       D7   G
Twenty-one years — but I got ninety-nine. *Chorus*

G
The train arrived, sixteen coaches long,
C   G
The train arrived, sixteen coaches long,

The train arrived, sixteen coaches long,
       D7   G
The girl I love is on that train and gone. *Chorus*

G
I looked down the track as far as I could see,
C   G
I looked down the track as far as I could see,

I looked down the track as far as I could see,
       D7   G
Little bitty hand was waving after me. *Chorus*

G
If anyone should ask you, who composed this song,
C   G
If anyone should ask you, who composed this song,

If anyone should ask you, who composed this song,
       D7   G
Tell him it was I, and I sing it all day long. *Chorus*

Poor Howard

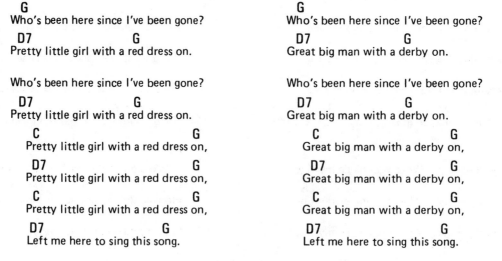

G
Who's been here since I've been gone?
D7   G
Pretty little girl with a red dress on.

Who's been here since I've been gone?
D7   G
Pretty little girl with a red dress on.
    C   G
Pretty little girl with a red dress on,
D7   G
Pretty little girl with a red dress on,
    C   G
Pretty little girl with a red dress on,
D7   G
Left me here to sing this song.

G
Who's been here since I've been gone?
D7   G
Great big man with a derby on.

Who's been here since I've been gone?
D7   G
Great big man with a derby on.
    C   G
Great big man with a derby on,
D7   G
Great big man with a derby on,
    C   G
Great big man with a derby on,
D7   G
Left me here to sing this song.

Roll In My Sweet Baby's Arms

Ain't gon - na work on the rail - road, _____ Ain't gon - na

work on the farm. _____ Well, I'll lay 'round the shack till the

mail train comes back, Then I'll roll in my sweet ba - by's arms. _____

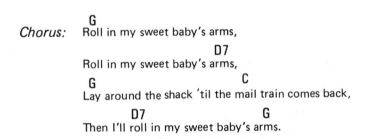

Chorus:
G
Roll in my sweet baby's arms,
D7
Roll in my sweet baby's arms,
G   C
Lay around the shack 'til the mail train comes back,
D7   G
Then I'll roll in my sweet baby's arms.

G
Can't see what's the matter with my true love,
D7
She done quit writing to me;
G   C
She must think I don't love her like I used to do,
D7   G
Ain't that a foolish idea. *Chorus*

G
Sometimes there's a change in the ocean;
D7
Sometimes there's a change in the sea;
G   C
Sometimes there's a change in my own true love;
D7   G
But there's never no change in me. *Chorus*

G
Mama's a ginger-cake baker;
D7
Sister can weave and can spin;
G   C
Dad's got an interest in that old cotton mill,
D7   G
Just watch that old money roll in. *Chorus*

G
They tell me that your parents do not like me;
D7
They have drove me away from your door;
G   C
If I had all my time to do over again,
D7   G
I would never go there any more. *Chorus*

G
Now where was you last Friday night,
D7
While I was locked up in jail;
G   C
Walking the streets with another man,
D7   G
Wouldn't even go my bail. *Chorus*

The Wabash Cannonball

Now the eastern states are dandies, so the western people say
From New York to St. Louis and Chicago by the way,
Thru the hills of Minnesota where the rippling waters fall
No chances can be taken on the Wabash Cannonball. *Chorus*

Here's to Daddy Claxton, may his name forever stand
May he be remembered through parts of all our land,
When his earthly race is over and the curtains round him fall,
We'll carry him on to glory on the Wabash Cannonball. *Chorus*

Katy Cline

Well now, who does not know Ka-ty Cline?_____ She

lives at the foot of the hill, _____ By the shad-y nook of some

old bab-bling brook, That runs by____ her dear old fa-ther's mill._____

Tell me that you love me, Ka-ty Cline, _____ Tell me that your

love's as true as mine._____ Tell me that you love your____

own tur-tle dove, Tell me that you love me, Ka-ty Cline. _____

G
It's way from my little cabin door,
D7
Oh it's way from my little cabin home.
G   **C**
There's no one to weep and there's no one to mourn
D7   **G**
And there's no one to see Katy Cline. *Chorus*

G
If I was a little bird,
D7
I'd never build my nest on the ground.
G   **C**
I'd build my nest in some high yonder tree
D7   **G**
Where them wild boys couldn't tear it down. *Chorus*

A MINOR CHORD

The Quartermaster Store

Guitar rhythm

There is beer, beer, beer that makes you feel so queer, In the store, in the store. There is beer, beer, beer that makes you feel so queer, In the quar - ter - mas - ter store. Mine eyes are __ dim, I can - not see, I have not __ brought my specs with me, __ I __ have not brought my specs with me.

G
There's a chief, chief, chief,

Who never brings us beef,
D7   G
In the store, in the store.

There's chief, chief, chief,

Who never brings us beef,
D7   G
In the Quartermaster Store. *Chorus*

. . .beans. . .make you fill your jeans. . .

. . .whisky. . .makes you feel so frisky. . .

. . .coke. . .makes you want to choke. . .

. . .tea. . .but not for you and me. . .

. . .bread. . .just like a lump of lead. . .

. . .soup. . .makes you want to poop. . .

. . .pie. . .that makes you want to cry. . .

. . .meat. . .that knocks you off your feet. . .

. . .chicken. . .the smell just makes you sicken. . .

. . .gravy. . .rejected by the navy. . .

. . .booze. . .to chase away the blues. . .

Nine-Pound Hammer

G

Ain't nobody's hammer in this mountain

C

D7   G

That rings like mine, that rings like mine. *Chorus*

G

Well I went up on the mountain just to see my baby

C

D7   G

And I ain't a-coming back, Lord, I ain't a-coming back. *Chorus*

G

It's a long way to Hazard, it's a long way to Harlan

C

D7   G

Just to get a little booze, just to get a little booze. *Chorus*

G

When I'm long gone you can make my tombstone

C

D7   G

Out of number nine coal, out of number nine coal. *Chorus*

Lesson 4
Key of E

E
B7
A

BASIC ARPEGGIO IN $\frac{3}{4}$

The arpeggio in $\frac{3}{4}$ is an extension of the four note arpeggio in $\frac{4}{4}$ time. The three quarter notes which normally make up a measure in $\frac{3}{4}$ time are now divided evenly into six eighth notes.

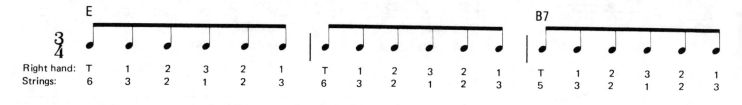

| Right hand: | T | 1 | 2 | 3 | 2 | 1 | | T | 1 | 2 | 3 | 2 | 1 | | T | 1 | 2 | 3 | 2 | 1 |
| Strings: | 6 | 3 | 2 | 1 | 2 | 3 | | 6 | 3 | 2 | 1 | 2 | 3 | | 5 | 3 | 2 | 1 | 2 | 3 |

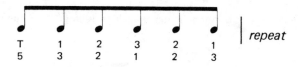

| T | 1 | 2 | 3 | 2 | 1 | *repeat* |
| 5 | 3 | 2 | 1 | 2 | 3 | |

We may alternate measures of "bass-chord-chord" and arpeggios. Be sure to time the whole sequence correctly so that the "one-two-three" of the bass-chord-chord strum and the "one-and two-and three-and" of the arpeggio are equal in total playing time.

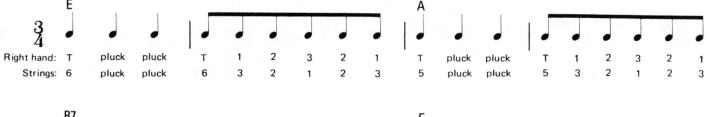

| Right hand: | T | pluck | pluck | T | 1 | 2 | 3 | 2 | 1 | T | pluck | pluck | T | 1 | 2 | 3 | 2 | 1 |
| Strings: | 6 | pluck | pluck | 6 | 3 | 2 | 1 | 2 | 3 | 5 | pluck | pluck | 5 | 3 | 2 | 1 | 2 | 3 |

| T | pluck | pluck | T | 1 | 2 | 3 | 2 | 1 | T | pluck | pluck | T | 1 | 2 | 3 | 2 | 1 |
| 5 | pluck | pluck | 5 | 3 | 2 | 1 | 2 | 3 | 6 | pluck | pluck | 6 | 3 | 2 | 1 | 2 | 3 |

Play these arpeggios with alternate basses.

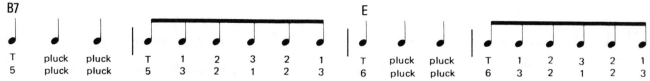

| Strings: | 6 | | 5 | | 5 | | 4 |

| | 4 | | 5 | | 6 | | 5 |

Down In The Valley

Down in the val - ley, Val - ley so low, Hang your head o - ver, Hear the wind blow.

E   B7
Hear the wind blow, love, hear the wind blow,
              E
Hang you head over, hear the wind blow.

E   B7
If you don't love me, love whom you please.
                E
Throw your arms 'round me, give my heart ease.

E   B7
Give my heart ease, love, give my heart ease,
                E
Throw your arms 'round me, give my heart ease.

E   B7   E   B7
Write me a letter, send it by mail,   As she rides by, love, as she rides by,
           E   E
Send it in care of the Birmingham Jail. So I can see her as she rides by.

E   B7   E   B7
Birmingham Jail, love, Birmingham Jail, Roses love sunshine, violets love dew,
           E   E
Send it in care of the Birmingham Jail. Angels in heaven know I love you.

E   B7   E   B7
Build me a castle forty feet high,   Know I love you, dear, know I love you,
           E   E
So I can see her as she rides by.   Angels in heaven know I love you.

Continue alternating measures of "bass-chord-chord" and arpeggios even if a chord change occurs in arpeggio measure.

Likes Likker Better Than Me

Based on a traditional song.
Additional Lyrics by
JERRY SILVERMAN

Oh, I'm in love with a brown-eyed boy, And he's in love with me, But he's in love with a whisky jug, Likes likker better than me.

Chorus
Oh, bring me back my brown-eyed boy, Oh, bring him back to me, Oh, bring me back, my brown-eyed boy, Likes likker better than me.

    E   A   E
Last night he came to see me again,
    B7   E
Last night he smiled on me,
               A   E
But tonight he smiles on a whisky jug,
    B7   E
Likes likker better than me. *Chorus*

    E   A   E
Sometimes I think I'll marry him,
    B7   E
For I love him dearer than life,
           A   E
But, oh, it's all so hard to bear
    B7   E
As a whisky drinker's wife. *Chorus*

    E   A   E
I think that I will say farewell
    B7   E
To my darling brown-eyed love.
        A   E
And if we ever meet again,
    B7   E
'Twill be in Heaven above. *Chorus*

Lydia Pinkham

Based on a traditional song.
Additional Lyrics by
JERRY SILVERMAN

Then __ we'll sing _____ of Lyd - i - a Pink - ham,

And __ her love _____ for the hu - man race; _____

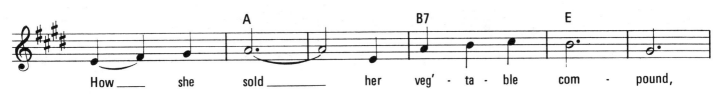

How __ she sold _____ her veg' - ta - ble com - pound,

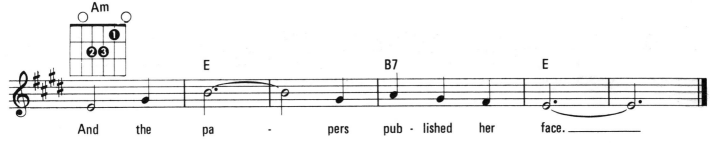

And the pa - pers pub - lished her face. _____

          E   A   B7   E
Chorus: Lydia Pinkham, Lydia Pinkham,
          B7   E
Let us sing her name in praise.
          A   B7   E
Lydia Pinkham, Lydia Pinkham,
Am   E   B7   E
For her compound brightens our days.

E A   B7   E
It is a mixture that's very tasty,
      B7   E
For it is made of vegetables pure.
      A   B7   E
And if you tell her what seems to ail you,
Am   E   B7   E
She will then prescribe you a cure. *Chorus*

E A   B7   E
Oh, it sells for a dollar a bottle,
      B7   E
Which is very cheap, you see.
      A B7   E
And if it doesn't cure you,
Am   E   B7   E
She will sell you six for three. *Chorus*

          E A   B7   E
Mrs. Jones, she had no children,
              B7   E
Though she loved them very dear.
          A   B7   E
So she bought some vegetable compound,
          Am   E   B7   E
Now she has them twice a year. *Chorus*

Away With Rum

We're com-ing, we're com-ing, our brave lit-tle band. On the right side of tem-p'rance we now take our stand. We don't use to-bac-co be-cause we do think, that the peo-ple who use it are like-ly to drink!

Chorus
A-way, A-way with rum, by gum, With rum, by gum; with rum___ by___ gum. A-way, A-way with rum, by gum; The song of the Sal-va-tion Ar-my.

E   B7   E
We never eat cookies because they have yeast,
          B7   E
And one little bite makes a man like a beast.
B7   E   B7   E
Oh, can you imagine a sadder disgrace
                    B7   E
Than a man in the gutter with crumbs on his face. *Chorus*

E   B7   E
We never eat fruitcake because it has rum,
          B7   E
And one little slice puts a man on the bum.
B7   E   B7   E
Oh can you imagine a sorrier sight
                    B7   E
Than a man eating fruitcake until he gets tight. *Chorus*

E   B7   E
When you go out dining, you're tempted to eat
          B7   E
All the delicacies on a menu elite,
          B7   E   B7   E
Remember this warning, on wine we've a ban,
                         B7   E
Try spaghetti and meat balls and not coq au vin. *Chorus*

E   B7   E
We don't allow backrubs, we think they're a crime,
                              B7   E
We will always condemn them in song and in rhyme;
B7   E   B7   E
An alcohol back rub is worse than straight gin,
                         B7   E
When you think of the liquor absorbed through your skin! *Chorus*

1-33

Bold Fisherman

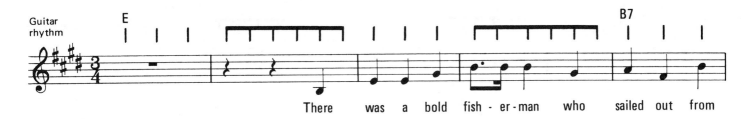

There was a bold fish-er-man who sailed out from

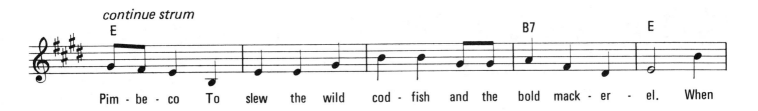

continue strum

Pim - be - co To slew the wild cod-fish and the bold mack-er - el. When

he ar-rived off Pim-be-co the storm-y winds did wild-ly blow, His lit - tle boat went

wib - ble wob - ble, And o - ver-board sprang he. "Twink - i doo - dle dum, twink - i

doo - dle dum," 'Twas the high - ly in - ter-est - ing song he sung. "Twink - i

doo - dle dum, twink - i doo - dle dum," Sang the bold fish - er - man.

E		B7 E		E		B7 E

He wriggled and scriggled in the water, so briny-O   His ghost walked at midnight to the bedside of his Mari-i-Jane.

He yellowed and bellowed for help but in vain.   He told her how dead he was; said she, "I'll go mad."

Then downward he did gently glide   "Since my lovey is so dead," said she,

To the bottom of the silvery tide;   "All joy on earth has fled for me;

But previously to this he cried   I never more will happy be."

"Fare thee well, Mar-i-Jane!" *Chorus*   And she went staring mad. *Chorus*

Rio Grande

And goodbye, fare you well, all you ladies of town,

Way, oh, Rio.

We've left you enough for to buy a silk gown.

And we're bound for the Rio Grande. *Chorus*

It's pack up your donkey and get under way,

Way, oh, Rio.

The girls we are leaving can take our half-pay,

And we're bound for the Rio Grande. *Chorus*

Now, you Bowery ladies, we'd have you to know,

Way, oh, Rio.

We're bound to the southward, Oh Lord, let us go,

And we're bound for the Rio Grande. *Chorus*

The Banks Of The Don

Canadian Folk Song

On the banks of the Don, there's a

dear lit - tle spot; A board - ing house prop - er, Where you get your meals

hot. You get fine bread and wa - ter and you won't pay a

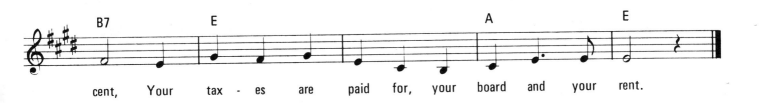

cent, Your tax - es are paid for, your board and your rent.

        E   A   E
So turn out every man of you, all in a line,
                                          B7
From the cell to the stoneyard you all must keep time,
        E   B7
You work like a Turk till the bell it strikes one,
            E   A   E
In that grand institution just over the Don.

            E   A   E
If you want to get into that palace so neat,
                                          B7
Take tanglefoot whisky and get drunk on the street,
        E   B7
You'll have a fine carriage to drive you from town
            E   A   E
To that grand institution just over the Don.

        E   A   E
Our boarders are honest, not one of them steals,
                                          B7
For we count all our knives and forks after each meal;
        E   B7
Our windows are airy and barred up beside
        E   A.   E
To keep our good boarders from falling outside.

            E   A   E
So turn out every man of you, all in a line,
                                          B7
From the cell to the stoneyard you all must keep time,
        E   B7
You work like a Turk till the bell it strikes one
                E   A   E
In that grand institution just over the Don.

Green Grow The Lilacs

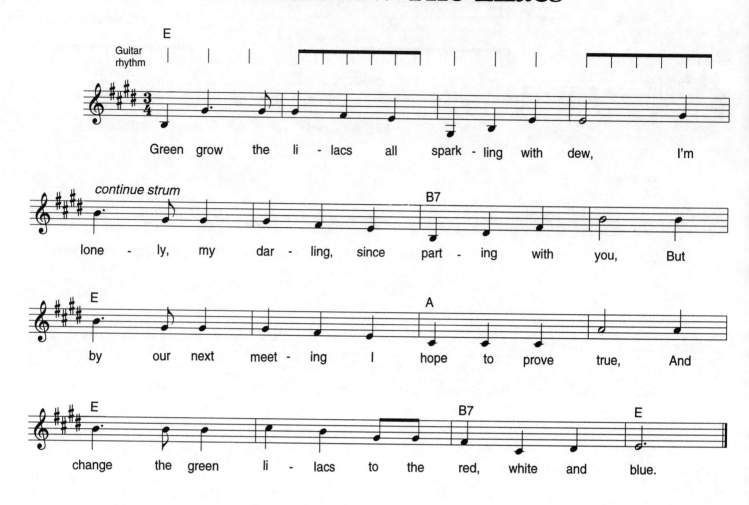

E
I used to have a sweetheart, but now I have none,
B7
Since she's gone and left me, I care not for one.
E   A
Since she's gone and left me, contented I'll be,
E   B7   E
For she loves another one better than me.

E
I passed my love's window, both early and late,
B7
The look that she gave me, it made my heart ache.
E   A
Oh, the look that she gave me was painful to see,
E   B7   E
For she loves another one better than me.

E
I wrote my love letters in rosy red lines,
B7
She sent me an answer all twisted in twines,
E   A
Saying, "Keep your love letters and I will keep mine,
E   B7   E
Just you write to your love and I'll write to mine."

Repeat Verse 1

Lesson 5
Key of C

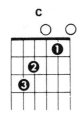 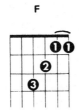 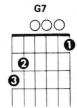

BRUSH STROKE

Strum downward quickly using the nails of fingers 1, 2 and 3. Your right wrist should make a short snapping movement.

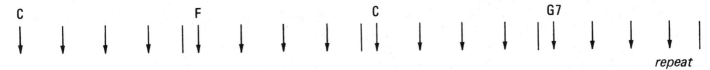

repeat

Now add a bass note with your thumb. The rhythm is the same as the bass-chord strum. The sound is different, due to the brushing fingernails.

repeat

After you have completed the downstroke bring the index finger upward over the first three strings. Now you must count to get the proper rhythm. "Thumb down-up" = "one two-and."

Alternate bass notes.

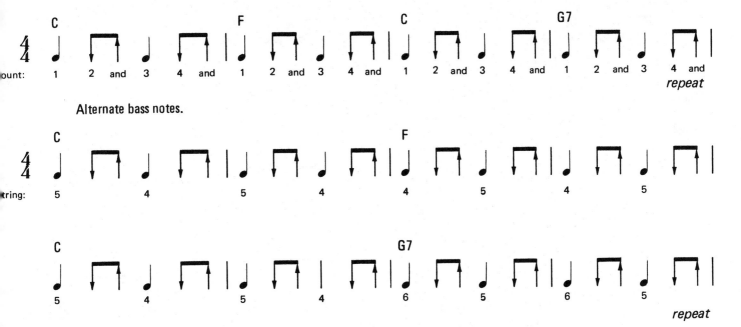

repeat

The Dodger Song

Oh, the can-di-date's a dodg-er, yes, a well-known dodg-er, Oh, the can-di-date's a dodg-er, yes, and I'm a dodg-er, too. He'll meet you and greet you and ask you for your vote, But look out, boys, — He's a-dodg-ing for a note. Yes, we're all ____ a-dodg-ing, A dodge, dodge, dodg-ing, Yes, we're all ____ a-dodg-ing out a way through the world.

C
Oh, the lawyer he's a dodger,
G7   C
yes, a well-known dodger,

Oh, the lawyer he's a dodger,
G7   C
yes, and I'm a dodger, too.

He'll plead your case and

claim you for a friend,
G7
But look out, boys, he's easy
C
for to bend! *Chorus*

C
Oh, the merchant he's a dodger,
G7   C
yes, a well-known dodger,

Oh, the merchant he's a dodger,
G7   C
yes, and I'm a dodger, too.

He'll sell you goods at

double the price,
G7
But when you go to pay him,
C
you'll have to pay him twice! *Chorus*

C
Oh, the farmer he's a dodger,
G7   C
yes, a well-known dodger,

Oh, the farmer he's a dodger,
G7   C
yes, and I'm a dodger, too.

He'll plow his cotton, he'll

hoe his corn,
G7
But he'll make a living just
C
as sure as you're born! *Chorus*

C
Oh, the lover he's a dodger,
G7   C
yes, a well-known dodger,

Oh, the lover he's a dodger,
G7   C
yes, and I'm a dodger, too.

He'll hug you and kiss you, and

call you his bride,
G7
But look out, girls, he's telling
C
you a lie! *Chorus*

1-39

Bed On The Floor

Based on a traditional song.
Additional Lyrics by
JERRY SILVERMAN

Chorus

Bed on the floor, ba-by; bed on the floor, ba-by.

Bed on the floor, ba-by; bed on the floor, And

I'll lay my head on the bed on the floor.

C
Make me a bed right down on the floor, baby,
F   C
Make me a bed right down on the floor;
  G7   C
And I'll lay my head on the bed on the floor. *Chorus*

C
Clock striking midnight, daylight to go, baby,
F   C
Clock striking midnight, daylight to go;
  G7   C
And I'll lay my head on the bed on the floor. *Chorus*

C
Sheriff on my trail with a big forty-four, baby,
F   C
Sheriff on my trail with a big forty-four;
  G7   C
And I'll lay my head on the bed on the floor. *Chorus*

C
In through the front and out the back door, baby,
F   C
In through the front and out the back door;
  G7   C
And I'll lay my head on the bed on the floor. *Chorus*

C
Next chance I get I'll even the score, baby,
F   C
Next chance I get I'll even the score;
  G7   C
And I'll lay my head on the bed on the floor. *Chorus*

In *Wildwood Flower* there are four brush strokes per measure. Follow the "guitar rhythm" carefully. Each quarter note gets one complete brush stroke.

Wildwood Flower

I will twine and will min - gle my wav - ing black hair With the

ros - es so red and the lil - ies so fair. The myr - tle so green of an

em - er - ald hue The pale em - a - ni - ta and is - lip so blue.

	C		G7	C
Oh, he promised to love me, he promised to love,
                                            G7   C
And to cherish me always all others above.
                                    F   C
I woke from my dream and my idol was clay.
                          G7   C
My passion for loving had vanished away.

             C   G7   C
Oh, he taught me to love him, he called me his flower,
                             G7   C
A blossom to cheer him through life's weary hour.
                   F   C
But now he is gone and left me alone,
                         G7   C
The wild flowers to weep and the wild birds to mourn.

    C   G7   C
I'll dance and I'll sing and my life shall be gay,
                         G7   C
I'll charm every heart in the crowd I survey;
                                 F   C
Though my heart now is breaking, he shall never know
                          G7   C
How his name makes me tremble, my pale cheeks to glow.

    C   G7   C
I'll dance and I'll sing and my heart shall be gay,
                         G7   C
I'll banish this weeping, drive troubles away.
                         F   C
I'll live yet to see him regret this dark hour,
                          G7   C
When he won and neglected this frail wildwood flower.

Tom Cat Blues

Guitar rhythm

I got an old tom cat; when he __ steps out

continue strum

all the puss - y cats __ in the neigh - bor - hood they be - gin to shout.

C
Here comes Ring Tail Tom,
G7
He's boss around the town,
C   F
And if you got your heat turned up,
C   G7   C
You better turn your damper down.

C
Ring Tail Tom on a fence,
G7
The old pussy cat on the ground,
C   F
Ring Tail Tom came off that fence,
C   G7   C
And they went round and round.

C
Lord, he's quick on the trigger,
G7
He's a natural-born crack shot,
C   F
He got a new target every night,
C   G7   C
And he sure does practice a lot.

C
He makes them roust about,
G7
He makes them roll their eyes,
C   F
They just can't resist my Ring Tail Tom,
C   G7   C
No matter how hard they tries;

C
You better watch old Ring Tail Tom,
G7
He's running around the town,
C   F
He won't have no pussy cats
C   G7   C
Come a-tomcattin' around.

C
Ring Tail Tom is the stuff,
G7
He's always running around;
C   F
All the pussy cats in the neighborhood
C   G7   C
Can't get old Ring Tail down;

C
He's always running around,
G7
Just can't be satisfied,
C   F
He goes out every night,
C   G7   C
With a new one by his side.

Camptown Races

by Stephen Foster

The long-tail filly and the big black hoss,
Doo-dah, doo-dah,
They fly the track and they both cut across,
Oh, doo-dah day.

The blind hoss sticken in a big mud hole,
Doo-dah, doo-dah,
Can't touch bottom with a ten-foot pole,
Oh, doo-dah day. *Chorus*

Old muley cow come onto the track,
Doo-dah, doo-dah,
The bobtail fling her over his back,
Oh, doo-dah day.

Then fly along like a railroad car,
Doo-dah, doo-dha,
Running a race with a shooting star,
Oh, doo-dah day. *Chorus*

See them flying on a ten-mile heat,
Doo-dah, doo-dah,
'Round the race track, then repeat,
Oh, doo-dah day.

I win my money on the bobtail nag,
Doo-dah, doo-dah,
I keep my money in an old towbag,
Oh, doo-dah day. *Chorus*

The Big Rock Candy Mountain

In the Big Rock Candy Mountain, boys,
You never change your socks.
And little streams of alkyhol
Come trickling down the rocks.
All the sheriffs have to tip their hats,
And the railroad bulls are blind.
There's a lake of stew,
And gingerale, too,
In the Big Rock Candy Mountain. *Chorus*

In the Big Rock Candy Mountain, boys,
The cops have wooden legs.
The bulldogs all have rubber teeth,
And the hens lay soft-boiled eggs.
The boxcars are all empty there,
And the sun shines every day.
I'm bound to go
Where there ain't no snow,
In the Big Rock Candy Mountain. *Chorus*

In the Big Rock Candy Mountain, boys,
The jails are made of tin.
And you can slip right out again,
Soon as they put you in.
There ain't no short-handled shovels there,
No axes, saws nor picks.
I'm bound to stay
Where they sleep all day,
In the Big Rock Candy Mountain. *Chorus*

Sailor On The Deep Blue Sea

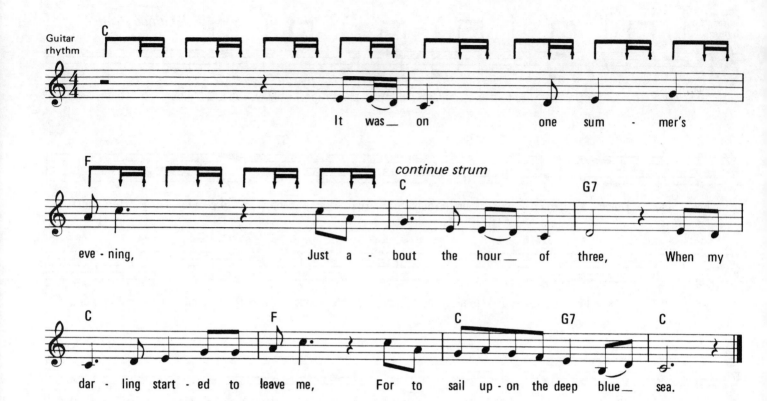

It was— on one sum-mer's eve-ning, Just a-bout the hour— of three, When my dar-ling start-ed to leave me, For to sail up-on the deep blue— sea.

C   F
How I cried the night we parted,
C   G7
Oh, it was so hard for me.
C   F
For I could not bear to think him
C   G7   C
A-sailing on the deep blue sea.

C   F
Oh, he promised to write me a letter
C   G7
He said he'd write to me
C   F
But I've not heard from my darling
C   G7   C
Who is sailing on the deep blue sea.

C   F
Perhaps a storm has drowned him,
C   G7
Perhaps he's untrue to me.
C   F
How can I know for certain,
C   G7   C
When no word comes from the deep blue sea?

C   F
Oh, my mother's dead and buried
C   G7
My pa's forsaken me
C   F
And I have no one for to love me
C   G7   C
But the sailor on the deep blue sea.

C   F
Farewell to friends and relations
C   G7
It's the last you'll see of me
C   F
For I'm going to end my troubles
C   G7   C
By drowning in the deep blue sea.

New River Train

Guitar rhythm

C

I'm rid - in' on that new riv - er train, I'm

continue strum
G7   C

rid - in' on that new riv - er train, Same old train that

F   C   G7   C

brought me here gon - na car - ry me back a - gain.

C
Honey, you can't love one,
         G7
Honey, you can't love one,
   C   F
You can't love one and have any fun,
C   G7   C
Honey, you can't love one.

C
Honey, you can't love two,
         G7
Honey, you can't love two,
   C   F
You can't love two and still be true,
C   G7   C
Honey, you can't love two.

C
Honey, you can't love three,
         G7
Honey, you can't love three,
   C   F
You can't love three and still love me,
C   G7   C
Honey, you can't love three.

C
Honey, you can't love four,
         G7
Honey, you can't love four,
   C   F
You can't love four or you'll want more,
C   G7   C
Honey, you can't love four.

C
Honey, you can't love five,
         G7
Honey, you can't love five,
   C   F
You can't love five and stay alive,
C   G7   C
Honey, you can't love five.

C
Honey, you can't love six,
         G7
Honey, you can't love six,
   C   F
You can't love six — don't try your tricks,
C   G7   C
Honey, you can't love six.

C
Honey, you can't love seven,
         G7
Honey, you can't love seven,
   C   F
You can't love seven and still go to heaven,
C   G7   C
Honey, you can't love seven.

C
Honey, you can't love eight,
         G7
Honey, you can't love eight,
   C   F
You can't love eight — now just you wait,
C   G7   C
Honey, you can't love eight.

C
Honey, you can't love nine,
         G7
Honey, you can't love nine,
   C   F
You can't love nine and still be mine,
C   G7   C
Honey, you can't love nine.

C
Honey, you can't love ten,
         G7
Honey, you can't love ten,
   C   F
You can't love ten, be they women or men,
C   G7   C
Honey, you can't love ten.

Repeat first verse

1-46

To the Student . . .

OK . . . So far so good.

Now we're going to put our newly acquired techniques to good and varied use. Coming up in Section Two is a mixed bag of song material in major and minor keys with a richer chord vocabulary than you've seen up to this point. After you've worked through all the songs and keys here, you will probably be hungry for additional material (available from Mel Bay Publications):

Action Songs for Children — *book*
America Sings! — *book*
The American History Songbook — *book*
American Love Songs & Ballads — *book*
Anyone Can Sing — *video*
Appalachian Folk Songs for Piano and Voice — *book*
The Backpacker's Songbook — *book*
Ballads & Songs of the Civil War — *book, tape, and CD*
Ballads & Songs of the Civil War for Guitar — *book*
Ballads & Songs of World War I — *book*
Mel Bay's Caroling Book — *book*
The Best of Vintage Dance — *book/CD set*
Blues Classics Songbook — *book*
Blues Guitar Songbook — *book*
The Robert Burns Songbook Volume 1 — *book*
Campfire Songbook — *book and tape*
Children Sing Around the World — *book*
Christmas Carols for Children — *book*
Complete Traditional Holiday Season Fake Book — *book*
Cowboy Songs, Jokes, Lingo & Lore — *book, tape and CD*
Crawdads, Doodlebugs & Creasy Greens — *book, tape and CD*
Dance of a Child's Dreams/Songs for Home & School — *book and CD*
John Dowland/The First Booke of Songes or Ayres — *book*
Early American Christmas Music — *book*
Early American Folk Hymns — *book*
Easiest Guitar Song Book — *book*
Family Carol Book — *book*
Favorite Carols Made Easy — *book*
Favourite English Carols --- *book*
Folk Songs for Schools & Camps — *book, tape and CD*
Folk Songs of the British Isles — *book*
Front Porch Old-Time Songbook — *book, tape, and CD*
Fun with Folk Songs — *book*
Great Irish Songs and Ballads Vol. 1 & 2 — *books*
The Green Grass Grew All Around — *book and CD*
Gypsy Songs of Russia & Hungary (Guitar-Vocal) — *book*
Gypsy Songs of Russia & Hungary (Piano-Vocal) — *book*
Helicon International Acoustic Tune Book — *book*
Immigrant Songbook — *book*
Ireland the Songs Vol. 1–4 — *books*
Ireland's Best Loved Songs and Ballads — *book*
Irish Session Tune Book — *book*
Italian Songs & Arias — *book*
Jewish Holiday Songs for Children — *book, tape, and CD*
Kidsongs — *book and tape*
Latin American Songs for Guitar — *book*
Le Hoogie Boogie Songbook — *book, tape, and CD*
The Light Crust Doughboys Songbook — *book/CD set*
Mallory and McCall's Irish Pub Songbook — *book*
Mandolin Songbook — *book*

Mexican Songs for Guitar — *book*
New Scottish Songbook — *book*
The Nineties Collection/New Scottish Tunes in Traditional Style —*book*
Old-Time Cowboy Songbook — *book*
Old-Time Gospel Songbook — *book, tape and CD*
100 Great Scottish Songs — *book/cassette set*
100 Irish Ballads Vol. 1 & 2 — *book/cassette sets*
Outlaw Ballads, Legends & Lore — *book,tape and CD*
Piano/Vocal Manuscript Book — *book*
Riders in the Sky/Saddle Pals — *book and CD*
The Salon Duo Collection Vol. 1 & 2 — *books*
Saltire Scottish Songbook — *book*
Simple Gifts — *book, tape, and CD*
Sing-Along Christmas Carols — *book*
Songs of the American People — *book*
Songs of Australia — *book*
Songs of the British Isles — *book*
Songs of the British Isles for Guitar — *book*
Songs of England — *book and tape*
Songs of France — *book*
Songs of Germany— *book*
Songs of the Great Outdoors — *book*
Songs of Ireland — *book and tape*
Songs of the Jazz Age — *book/CD set*
Songs of the Jewish People — *book*
Songs of Latin America — *book*
Songs of Mexico — *book and tape*
Songs of the Ragtime Era — *book/CD set*
Songs of Scotland — *book and tape*
Songs of the Sea, Rivers, Lakes & Canals — *book*
Songs of Spain/Piano-Vocal — *book*
Songs We Love to Sing, Book 1 & 2 — *books*
Songs of the Western Frontier — *book*
Songs of the Wild West — *book*
Song Writer's Manuscript Book — *book*
Spanish Songs for Guitar — *book*
Tender Shepherd — *book, tape and CD*
The Titanic Songbook — *book and CD*
Titanic Tunes/"Songs from Steerage" — *book*
Train Songs — *book*
Treasures of Tin Pan Alley — *book and tape*
A Tribute to Carolan — *book*
Turkey in the Straw — *book, tape and CD*
Vaudeville Favorites — *book and CD*
The Very Best of Foster & Allen — *book*
The World Turned Upside Down — *book, tape and CD*
You Can Teach Yourself® Folk Singing Guitar — *book*
You Can Teach Yourself® to Sing — *book, tape, and CD*
You Can Teach Yourself® Song Writing — *book and CD*

Contents—Section Two

Basic Guitar Chords
(As Learned in Section One)

D

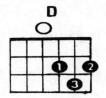

A

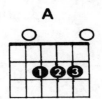

G

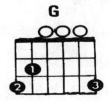

E

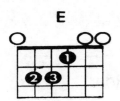

C

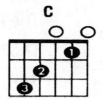

F

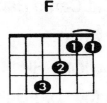

A7

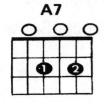

E7

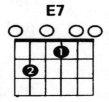

D7

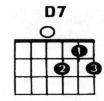

B7

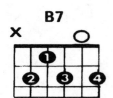

G7

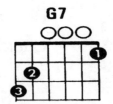

Am

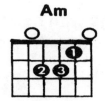

Basic Strums

The right-hand strums on the next two pages were introduced in Book One of *Look—Listen And Learn*. Each one was illustrated with a number of songs.

The Thumb-Finger Pluck

Finger a G chord.

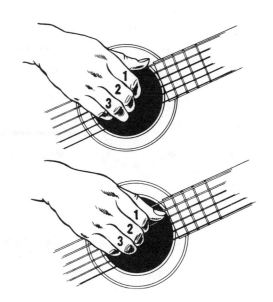

Rest the thumb on the sixth string and bring the tips of fingers one, two and three into contact lightly with strings three, two and one, respectively.

Thumb strikes sixth string. . .followed by. . .the three fingers plucking upward together on the first three strings.

Try the same pattern with a D chord (thumb on fourth string) and an A7 (thumb on fifth string).

THREE-QUARTER TIME

The accompaniment for a song in three-quarter time is quite simple. It is merely an exension of the basic thumb-finger pluck into a thumb-finger-finger pluck.

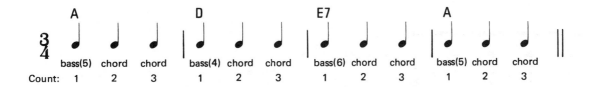

A			D			E7			A		
bass(5)	chord	chord	bass(4)	chord	chord	bass(6)	chord	chord	bass(5)	chord	chord

Count: 1 2 3 1 2 3 1 2 3 1 2 3

Basic Arpeggio In 4/4 Time

The fingers of the right hand may pluck the strings one at a time in various patterns and combinations. Chords played in this manner are called *arpeggios*.

First, finger a G chord and move the fingers of the right hand as follows:

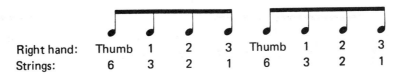

Right hand:	Thumb	1	2	3	Thumb	1	2	3
Strings:	6	3	2	1	6	3	2	1

Try this same movement with other chords.

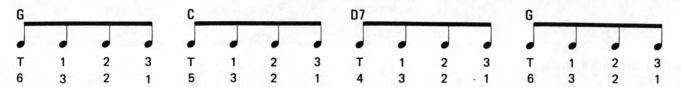

G				C				D7				G			
T	1	2	3	T	1	2	3	T	1	2	3	T	1	2	3
6	3	2	1	5	3	2	1	4	3	2	1	6	3	2	1

Now we will add two quarter notes—the usual bass-chord strum—*before* the four eighth notes of the arpeggio. Be sure to time the whole sequence correctly so that the "one-two" of the bass-chord strum and the "three-and-four-and" of the arpeggio are equal in total playing time.

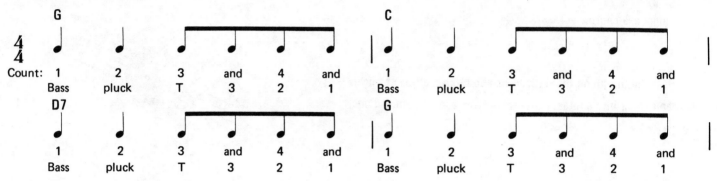

Basic Arpeggio In 3/4 Time

The arpeggio in $\frac{3}{4}$ is an extension of the four-note arpeggio in $\frac{4}{4}$ time. The three quarter notes which normally make up a measure in $\frac{3}{4}$ time are now divided evenly into six eighth notes.

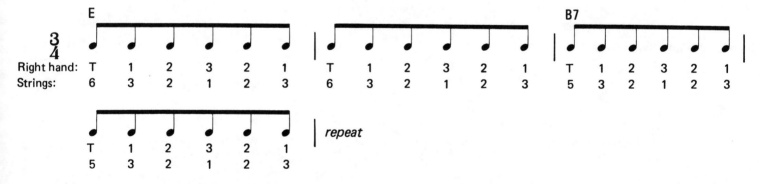

We may alternate measures of "bass-chord-chord" and arpeggios. Be sure to time the whole sequence correctly so that the "one-two-three" of the bass-chord-chord strum and the "one-and-two-and-three-and" of the arpeggio are equal in total playing time.

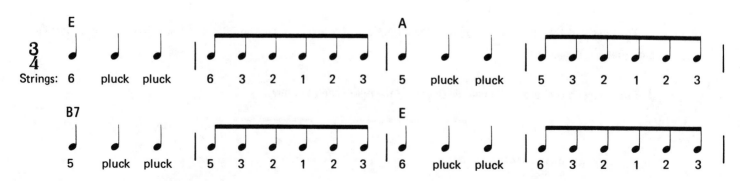

Brush Stroke

Strum downward quickly using the nails of fingers 1, 2 and 3. Your right wrist should make a short snapping movement.

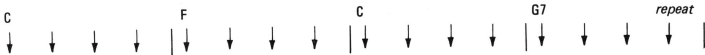

Now add a bass note with your thumb. The rhythm is the same as the bass-chord strum. The sound is different, due to the brushing fingernails.

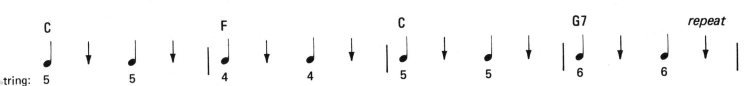

After you have completed the downstroke bring the index finger upward over the first three strings. Now you must count to get the proper rhythm. "Thumb down-up" = "one two-and."

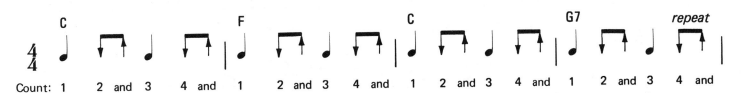

Minor Keys

Songs in minor keys do not always follow the neat chord progressions that we see in songs in major keys. For example, if we consider a typical folk song in the key of A major we may be fairly certain that we will encounter the chords A, D and E7. These chords are based on the first, fourth and fifth notes of the scale of A major. This *I, IV, V* relationship holds true, by the same token, for all major keys. In C we get C, F, G7. In G we get G, C, D7. In D we get D, G, A7. In E we get E, A, B7.

This I, IV, V regularity is only sometimes found in songs in minor keys. As you will see in the songs in this section there is a great deal of diversity among minor key songs. No simple predictable pattern emerges out of which we may construct a "table of chords." Rather, each song will have to be taken individually. We will see that the V chord is sometimes minor and sometimes major (that is V7 as in major keys). The IV may likewise be either major or minor. In addition, there are to be found III and VI chords (such as C and F in A minor). Another very common chord which takes on the function of the dominant chord (that is, the V) is the VII (G in A minor).

So, we will take each song as we come to it—learning whatever new chords we need as we go along.

SONGS IN A MINOR

Katy Cruel

A minor   E minor

Suggested strum: Brush Stroke

Verse

Am ... Em ... Am ... Em

When I first came to town, They called me "the Rov-ing Jew-el."

F ... C ... Em ... C

Now they've changed their tune And call me "Ka-ty Cru-el."

Chorus

Em ... Am ... Em ... Am ... E7 ... Am

Oh, did-dle lul-ly day, Oh, de lit-tle li-o day.

Am ... Em ... Am ... Em

Oh, that I was where I would be, Then should I be where I am not;

F ... C ... Em ... C

Here I am where I must be, Where I would be I can not;

Em ... Am ... Em ... Am ... E7 ... Am

Oh, did-dle lul-ly day, Oh, de lit-tle li-o day.

Am   Em
I know whom I love,

Am   Em
I know who does love me,

F   C
I know where I'll go,

Em   C
And I know who'll come with me. *Chorus*

Am   Em
Through the woods I'll go,

Am   Em
Through the boggy mire,

F   C
Straightway on the road,

Em   C
Till I come to my heart's desire. *Chorus*

Am   Em
Eyes as black as coal,

Am   Em
Lips as red as cherry,

F   C
And 'tis her delight

Em   C
To make the young folks merry. *Chorus*

Hudson River Steamboat

D minor

Suggested strum: Brush Stroke

Am ... **E7** ... **Am**

Hud - son Riv - er steam - boat, steam - ing up and down, New York to Al - ba - ny or

E7 ... **Am** ... **Dm** ... **E7**

an - y riv - er town, Choo, choo to go a - head, choo, choo to slack 'er, The

Am ... **E7** ... **Am** ... Chorus **C**

cap - tain and the first mate they both chew to - bac - co. Choo, choo to go a - head,

G7 ... **C** ... **G7** ... **C**

Choo, choo to slack 'er, Pack - et boat, tow boat and a dou - ble stack - er.

F ... **C** ... **F** ... **C**

Choo, choo to Tar - ry Town, Spuy - ten Duy - vil, all a - round,

G7 ... **C**

Choo, choo to go a - head, Choo, choo to back 'er.

Am   **E7**   **Am**
Shad boat, pickle boat, lying side by side,
       E7   **Am**
Fisherfolk and sailormen, waiting for the tide,
       Dm   **E7**
Rain cloud, storm cloud over yonder hill,
Am   **E7**   **Am**
Thunder on the Dunderberg, rumbles in the kill. *Chorus*
	Am **E7** **Am**
	The Sedgewick was racing and she lost all hope,
	       E7 **Am**
	Used up her steam on the big calliope,
	       Dm **E7**
	But she hopped right along, she was hopping quick,
	Am **E7** **Am**
	All the way from Stony Point to Pappaloppen Crick. *Chorus*

Final Chorus
C
Choo, choo to go ahead,
     G7
Choo, choo to slack 'er,
C   **G7**   **C**
Packet boat, tow boat and a double stacker.
F   **C**   **F**   **C**
New York to Albany, Rondout and Tivoli,

Choo, choo to go ahead,
     G7   **C**
And choo, choo to back 'er.

The Bonnie Ship, The Diamond

Suggested strum: Brush Stroke

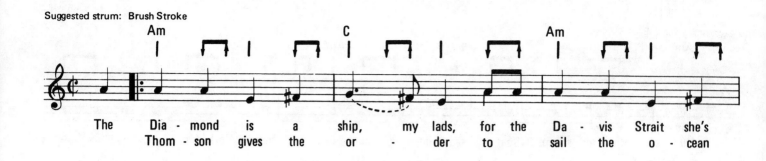

The Dia - mond is a ship, my lads, for the Da - vis Strait she's
Thom - son gives the or - der to sail the o - cean

bound, And the quay it is all gar - nish - ed with bon - nie lass - es
wide, where the sun it nev - er sets, my lads, no dark - ness dims __ the

1. Am
2. Am   Chorus   Am   G   Am

round. Cap - tain sky. So it's cheer up, my lads, let your hearts nev - er

G   Am   G   Am   G   Am

fail While the bon - nie ship, The Dia - mond goes a - fish - ing for the whale.

Am	C
Along the quay at Peterhead, the

Am	Em
lasses stand around,

Am	C
Wi' their shawls all pulled about them

E7	Am
and the salt tears runnin' down;

C
Don't you weep, my bonnie lass,

Am	Em
though you be left behind,

Am	C
For the rose will grow on Greenland's

E7	Am
ice before we change our mind. *Chorus*

Am	C
Here's a health to The Resolution,

Am	Em
likewise the Eliza Swan,

Am	C
Here's a health to The Battler of

E7	Am
Montrose and The Diamond, ship of fame;

C
We wear the trousers of the white

Am	Em
and the jackets o' the blue,

Am	C
When we return to Peterhead we'll

E7	Am
have sweethearts enoo. *Chorus*

Am	C
It will be bright both day and night when

Am	Em
the Greenland lads come home,

Am	C
Wi' a ship that's full o' oil, my lads,

E7	Am
and money to our name;

C
We'll make the cradles for to rock

Am	Em
and the blankets for to tear.

Am	C
And every lass in Peterhead sing

E7	Am
"Hushabye, my dear." *Chorus*

Haul Away, Joe

Suggested strum: Thumb-finger Pluck

In measures 4 and 8 brush down over the D minor and E7 chords with your thumb and then resume the bass-chord, thumb-finger pluck on the A minor.

Now, when I was a little lad, me mother always told me,
       Am   Em   Dm E7 Am

Am   Em   Dm   Em
Now, when I was a little lad, me mother always told me,
Am   Em   Dm E7 Am
Way, haul away, we'll haul away, Joe.
Em   Dm   Em
That if I didn't kiss the girls, me lips would grow all mouldy,
Am   Em   Dm E7 Am
Way, haul away, we'll haul away, Joe. *Chorus*

Am   Em   Dm   Em
King Louis was the king of France before the Revolution,
Am   Em   Dm E7 Am
Way, haul away, we'll haul away, Joe.
Em   Dm   Em
But then he got his head cut off, which spoiled his constitution,
Am   Em   Dm E7 Am
Way, haul away, we'll haul away, Joe. *Chorus*

Am   Em   Dm   Em
Once I had a scolding wife, she wasn't very civil,
Am   Em   Dm E7 Am
Way, haul away, we'll haul away, Joe.
Em   Dm   Em
I clapped a plaster on her mouth and sent her to the divil,
Am   Em   Dm E7 Am
Way, haul away, we'll haul away, Joe. *Chorus*

Am   Em   Dm   Em
Way, haul away, we'll haul for better weather,
Am   Em   Dm E7 Am
Way, haul away, we'll haul away, Joe.
Em   Dm   Em
Way, haul away, we'll haul and hang together,
Am   Em   Dm E7 Am
Way, haul away, we'll haul away, Joe. *Chorus*

Tobacco's But An Indian Weed

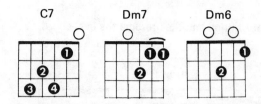

Suggested strum: All arpeggios in measures where there are either one or two chords. In measures where there are three chords, continue the arpeggios where possible and follow the arrows for brush strokes where indicated. In four-chord measures, play all down brush strokes.

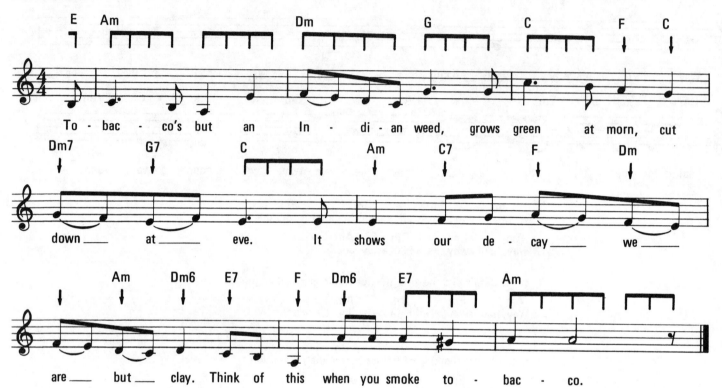

To - bac - co's but an In - di - an weed, grows green at morn, cut down ___ at ___ eve. It shows our de - cay ___ we ___ are ___ but ___ clay. Think of this when you smoke to - bac - co.

E Am   Dm G
The pipe that is so lily-white,

  C   F C Dm7 G7 C
Wherein so many take delight,

   Am C7 F
Gone with a touch;

Dm   Am Dm6
Man's life is such,

E7   F Dm6   E7   Am
Think of this when you smoke tobacco.

E Am   Dm G
The pipe that is so foul within,

  C   F C Dm7 G7 C
Shows how the soul is stained with sin;

   Am C7 F
It doth require

Dm   Am Dm6
The purging fire,

E7   F Dm6   E7   Am
Think of this when you smoke tobacco.

E Am   Dm G
The ashes that are left behind,

  C   F C Dm7 G7 C
Do serve to put us all in mind,

   Am C7 F
That unto dust,

Dm   Am Dm6
Return we must,

E7   F Dm6   E7   Am
Think of this when you smoke tobacco.

E Am   Dm G
The smoke that doth so high ascend,

  C   F C Dm7 G7 C
Shows that our life must have an end;

   Am C7 F
The vapour's gone,

Dm   Am Dm6
Man's life is done,

E7   F Dm6   E7   Am
Think of this when you smoke tobacco.

SONGS IN E MINOR
The Cat Came Back

Suggested Strum: Thumb-finger Pluck

Old Mis-ter John-son had trou-bles of his own, He had a yel-low cat which would-n't leave its home; He tried and he tried to give the cat a-way, He gave it to a man go-ing far, far a-way.

Chorus

But the cat came back the ver-y next day, The cat came back, they thought he was a gon-er but the cat came back, It just could-n't stay a-way.

Em	D	C	B7

The man around the corner swore he'd kill the cat on sight,

| Em | D | C | B7 |

He loaded up his shotgun with nails and dynamite;

| Em | D | C | B7 |

He waited and he waited for the cat to come around,

| Em | D | C | B7 |

Ninety-seven pieces of the man is all they found. *Chorus*

| Em | D | C | B7 |

He gave it to a little boy with a dollar note,

| Em | D | C | B7 |

Told him for to take it up the river in a boat;

| Em | D | C | B7 |

They tied a rope around its neck, it must have weighed a pound,

| Em | D | C | B7 |

Now they drag the river for a little boy that's drowned. *Chorus*

| Em | D | C | B7 |

He gave it to a man going up in a balloon,

| Em | D | C | B7 |

He told him for to take it to the man in the moon,

| Em | D | C | B7 |

The balloon came down about ninety miles away,

| Em | D | C | B7 |

Where he is now, well I dare not say. *Chorus*

| Em | D | C | B7 |

He gave it to a man going way out west,

| Em | D | C | B7 |

Told him for to take it to the one he loved the best;

| Em | D | C | B7 |

First the train hit the curve, then it jumped the rail,

| Em | D | C | B7 |

Not a soul was left behind to tell the gruesome tale. *Chorus*

| Em | D | C | B7 |

Away across the ocean they did send the cat at last,

| Em | D | C | B7 |

Vessel only out a day and taking water fast;

| Em | D | C | B7 |

People all began to pray, the boat began to toss,

| Em | D | C | B7 |

A great big gust of wind came by and every soul was lost. *Chorus*

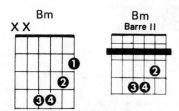

Santy Anno

In order to play the barre properly, lay your 1st finger flat over all six strings.

Press hard without bending if possible. Then place the other fingers.

Suggested Strum: Brush Stroke

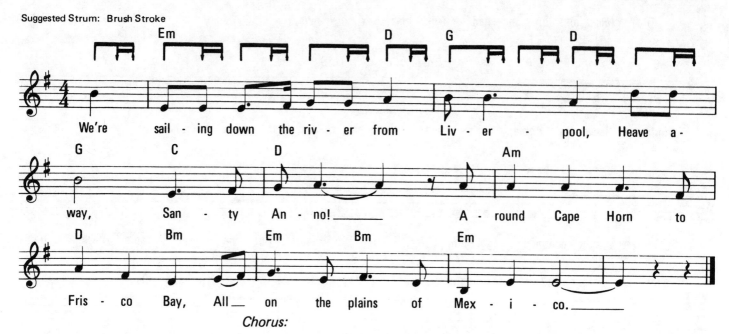

We're sail-ing down the riv-er from Liv-er-pool, Heave a-way, San-ty An-no! A-round Cape Horn to Fris-co Bay, All on the plains of Mex-i-co.

Chorus:

Em   D G D
So heave her up and away we go,

    G   C   D
Heave away, Santy Anno!

Am   D Bm
Heave her up and away we go,

    Em Bm   Em
All on the plains of Mexico.

Em   D G   D
She's a fast clipper ship and a bully good crew,

    G   C   D
Heave away, Santy Anno!

Am   D Bm
A down-east Yankee for her captain, too,

    Em Bm   Em
All on the plains of Mexico. *Chorus*

Em   D G   D
There's plenty of gold, so I've been told,

    G   C   D
Heave away, Santy Anno!

   Am   D Bm
There's plenty of gold, so I've been told,

    Em Bm   Em
All on the plains of Mexico. *Chorus*

Em   D G   D
Back in the days of forty-nine,

    G   C   D
Heave away, Santy Anno!

Am   D   Bm
Those were the days of the good old time,

    Em Bm   Em
All on the plains of Mexico. *Chorus*

Em   D G   D
When Zachary Taylor gained the day,

    G   C   D
Heave away, Santy Anno!

   Am   D Bm
He made poor Santy run away,

    Em Bm   Em
All on the plains of Mexico. *Chorus*

Em   D G   D
Santy Anno was a good old man,

    G   C   D
Heave away, Santy Anno!

  Am   D Bm
Till he got into war with Uncle Sam,

    Em Bm   Em
All on the plains of Mexico. *Chorus*

The Bullgine Run

Oh, the smart-est clip-per you can find, Ah hee, ah ho, are you most done? Is the Marg-'ret Ev-ans of the Blue Cross line, So clear a-way the track, let the bull-gine run.

Chorus

To my hey rig a jig in a low-back car, Ah hee, ah ho, are you most done? With Li-za Lee all on my knee, So clear a-way the track, let the bull-gine run.

Em   D   Em   Bm
Oh, the Marg'ret Evans of the Blue Cross Line,
   G   Bm
  Ah hee, ah ho, are you most done?
Em   D
She's never a day behind her time,
    Em   B7   Em
So clear away the track, let the bullgine run. *Chorus*
	Em D Em Bm
	We work like hell for a dollar a day,
	   G Bm
	  Ah hee, ah ho, are you most done?
	Em D
	When we get home we spend our pay,
	    Em B7 Em
	So clear away the track, let the bullgine run. *Chorus*

Em   D Em Bm
Oh, it's when I come home across the sea,
   G   Bm
  Ah hee, ah ho, are you most done?
Em   D
It's Liza, will you marry me?
    Em   B7   Em
So clear away the track, let the bullgine run. *Chorus*
	Em D Em Bm
	If Liza Lee should turn me down,
	   G Bm
	  Ah hee, ah ho, are you most done?
	Em D
	It's good-bye, boys, I'm outward bound,
	    Em B7 Em
	So clear away the track, let the bullgine run. *Chorus*

Didn't My Lord Deliver Daniel?

Suggested Strums:
  Brush Stroke for Chorus
  Bass-chord arpeggio for Verse

Am
The moon run down in a purple stream,

Em
The sun forbear to shine.

Am   Em
And every star will disappear,

A7   B7   Em
King Jesus shall be mine. *Chorus*

Am
I set my foot on the Gospel ship,

Em
And the ship began for to sail.

Am   Em
It landed me over on Canaan's shore,

A7   B7   Em
I know I will never fail. *Chorus*

Go Down, Moses

Suggested Strum: Arpeggios

"Thus spoke the Lord," bold Moses said,
   Em   B7   Em

B7   Em
Let my people go.

        B7   Em
"If not, I'll strike your first born dead,"

B7   Em
Let my people go. *Chorus*

        Em   B7   Em
"Your foes shall not before you stand,"

B7   Em
Let my people go.

        B7   Em
"And you'll possess fair Canaan's land,"

B7   Em
Let my people go. *Chorus*

        Em   B7   Em
"You'll not get lost in the wilderness,"

B7   Em
Let my people go.

        B7 Em
"With a lighted candle in your breast,"

B7   Em
Let my people go. *Chorus*

SONGS IN D MINOR
What Shall We Do With The Drunken Sailor?

Suggested Strum: Brush Stroke

Dm What shall we do with the drunk-en sail-or? **C** What shall we do with the drunk-en sail-or?

Dm What shall we do with the drunk-en sail-or, **C** Ear-lye in the **Dm** morn-ing?

Chorus

Dm Hoo-ray, and up she ris-es, **C** Hoo-ray, and up she ris-es,

Dm Hoo-ray, and up she ris-es, **C** Ear-lye in the **Dm** morn-ing.

Dm
Put him in the scuppers with a hose-pipe on him,
C
Put him in the scuppers with a hose-pipe on him,
Dm
Put him in the scuppers with a hose-pipe on him,
C   **Dm**
Earlye in the morning. *Chorus*

Dm
Put him in the life boat till he's sober,
C
Put him in the life boat till he's sober,
Dm
Put him in the life boat till he's sober,
C   **Dm**
Earlye in the morning. *Chorus*

Dm
Heave him by the leg in a running bowline,
C
Heave him by the leg in a running bowline,
Dm
Heave him by the leg in a running bowline,
C   **Dm**
Earlye in the morning. *Chorus*

Dm
Shave his belly with a rusty razor,
C
Shave his belly with a rusty razor,
Dm
Shave his belly with a rusty razor,
C   **Dm**
Earlye in the morning. *Chorus*

Dm
That's what we'll do with a drunken sailor,
C
That's what we'll do with a drunken sailor,
Dm
That's what we'll do with a drunken sailor,
C   **Dm**
Earlye in the morning. *Chorus*

Cod-Liver Oil

G minor   Gm
Barre III

Suggested Strum: 3/4 Arpeggios

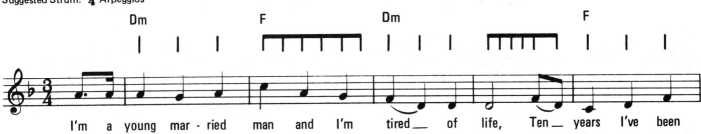

I'm a young mar-ried man and I'm tired__ of life, Ten__ years I've been

wed to a pale sick-ly wife; She has noth-ing to do on-ly

sit down and cry   Pray-ing, oh pray-ing to God she could die.

Dm	F	Dm

A friend of me own came to see me one day,

F   **Gm**   **Dm**
I told him my wife she was pining away;

    Am   **F**   **Am**
He afterwards told me that she would get strong

Dm   **Am**   **Dm**
If I'd get a bottle from dear Doctor John.

Dm   **F**   **Dm**
I bought her a bottle 'twas just for a try,

F   **Gm**   **Dm**
The way that she drank it, I thought she would die;

    Am   **F**   **Am**
I bought her another, it vanished the same

Dm   **Am**   **Dm**
And then she took cod-liver oil on the brain.

Dm   **F**   **Dm**
I bought her another, she drank it no doubt,

F   **Gm**   **Dm**
Then owing to that oil she got terribly stout;

    Am   **F**   **Am**
And when she got stout, then of course she got strong

Dm   **Am**   **Dm**
And then I got jealous of dear Doctor John.

Dm   **F**   **Dm**
Oh doctor, oh doctor, oh dear Doctor John,

F   **Gm**   **Dm**
Your cod-liver oil is so pure and so strong;

    Am   **F**   **Am**
I'm afraid of me life, I'll go down to the soil

Dm   **Am**   **Dm**
If my wife don't stop drinking your cod-liver oil.

    Dm   **F**   **Dm**
Our house it resembles a big doctor's shop,

    F   **Gm**   **Dm**
It is covered with bottles from bottom to top;

      Am   **F**   **Am**
And early in the morning when the kettle do boil

    Dm   **Am**   **Dm**
You'd swear it was singing of cod-liver oil.

Henry Martin

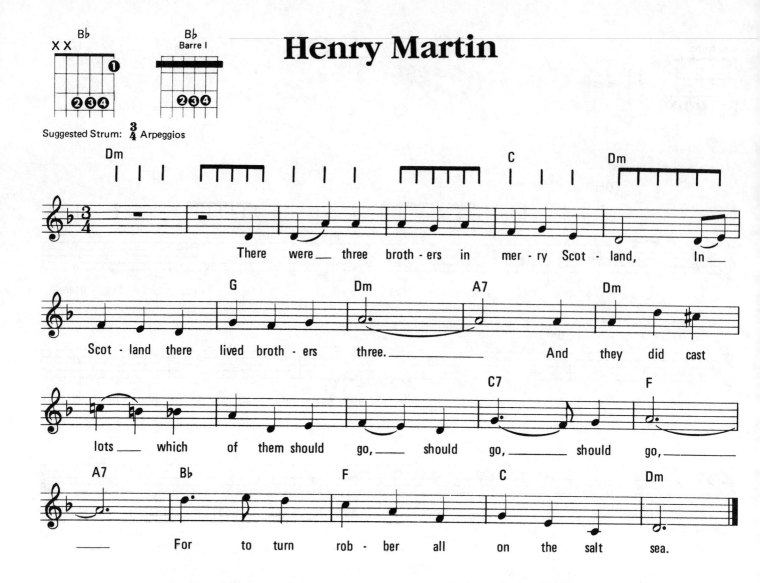

Dm There were __ three broth-ers in **C** mer-ry Scot-land, **Dm** In __

G Scot-land there lived broth-ers **Dm** three. _____ **A7** And they did **Dm** cast

lots __ which of them should go, __ should **C7** go, _____ should **F** go, _____

A7 __ **Bb** For to turn rob-ber all **F** on the salt **C** sea. **Dm**

Dm   C   Dm
The lot it fell upon Henry Martin,
          G   Dm A7
The youngest of all the three,
    Dm
That he should turn robber all on the salt sea,
          C7   F A7
     salt sea, salt sea.
Bb   F   C   Dm
For to maintain his two brothers and he.
    Dm   C   Dm
He had not been sailing but a long winter's night,
          G   Dm A7
And part of a short winter's day,
    Dm   C7   F A7
When he espi-ed a lofty stout ship, stout ship, stout ship,
Bb   F   C   Dm
Come a-bibbing down on him straightway.
    Dm   C   Dm
"Hello, hello," cried Henry Martin,
          G   Dm A7
"What makes you sail so nigh?"
    Dm
"I'm a rich merchant ship bound for fair London Town,
          C7   F A7
     London Town, London Town,
Bb   F   C   Dm
Will you please for to let me pass by?"

Dm   C   Dm
"Oh no, oh no," cried Henry Martin,
          G   Dm A7
"That thing it never can be,
    Dm   C7   F A7
For I have turned robber all on the salt sea, salt sea, salt sea,
Bb   F   C   Dm
For to maintain my two brothers and me"
    Dm   C   Dm
With broadside and broadside and at it they went
          G   Dm A7
For fully two hours or three,
    Dm   C7
Till Henry Martin gave to her the death shot, the death shot,
          F A7
     the death shot,
Bb   F   C   Dm
Heavily listing to starboard went she.
    Dm   C   Dm
Bad news, bad news to old England came,
          G   Dm A7
Bad news to fair London Town.
    Dm
There was a rich merchant and she's cast away,
          C7   F A7
     cast away, cast away,
Bb   F   C   Dm
And with all of her merry men drowned.

2-18

Hieland Laddie

Suggested Strum: Thumb-finger Pluck

Dm ... **Gm** ... **Dm** ... **Gm** ... **Dm**

Was you ev - er in Que - bec?___ Bon - nie Lad - die,

Gm ... **C** ... **F** ... **C7** ... **A7**

Hie - land Lad - die Stow - ing tim - ber on the deck,___ My

Chorus

Dm ... **C** ... **Dm** ... **Bb** ... **Am**

bon - nie Hie - land Lad - die. Hey, ho, and a -

C7 ... **F** ... **Gm** ... **Dm** ... **Gm** ... **C**

way we go. Bon - nie Lad - die, Hie - land Lad - die,

Bb **Am** ... **C7** ... **A7** ... **Dm** ... **C** ... **Dm**

Hey, ho, and a - way we go, my bon - nie Hie - land Lad - die.

Dm   **Gm Dm**
Was you ever in Callao?
Gm **Dm** **Gm**   **C**
Bonnie Laddie, Hieland Laddie
  F   **C7** **A7**
Where the girls are never slow,
  Dm   **C**   **Dm**
My bonnie Hieland Laddie. *Chorus*

Dm   **Gm Dm**
Was you ever in Baltimore?
Gm **Dm** **Gm**   **C**
Bonnie Laddie, Hieland Laddie
  F   **C7** **A7**
Dancing on that sanded floor,
  Dm   **C**   **Dm**
My bonnie Hieland Laddie. *Chorus*

Dm   **Gm Dm**
Was you ever in Mobile Bay?
Gm **Dm** **Gm**   **C**
Bonnie Laddie, Hieland Laddie
  F   **C7** **A7**
Screwing cotton by the day,
  Dm   **C**   **Dm**
My bonnie Hieland Laddie. *Chorus*

Dm   **Gm Dm**
Was you on the Brummalow?
Gm **Dm** **Gm**   **C**
Bonnie Laddie, Hieland Laddie
   F   **C7** **A7**
Where Yankee boys are all the go,
  Dm   **C**   **Dm**
My bonnie Hieland Laddie. *Chorus*

Dm   **Gm Dm**
Was you ever in Dundee?
Gm **Dm** **Gm**   **C**
Bonnie Laddie, Hieland Laddie
  F   **C7** **A7**
There some pretty ships you see,
  Dm   **C**   **Dm**
My bonnie Hieland Laddie. *Chorus*

High Germany

Suggested Strum: Bass-chord Arpeggios

O Pol-ly dear, O Pol-ly, the rout has now be-gun, and we must march a-way at the beat-ing of the drum. Go dress your-self all in your best and come a-long with me, I'll take you to the cru-el wars in High Ger-ma-ny.

```
        Dm C Dm   F   Gm          Dm
I'll buy you a horse, my love, and on it you shall ride,
        F   C7  F Bb  F   C7    F C7
And all of my delight shall be riding by your side;
        F   Gm  F Bb    Am      Bb    C
We'll call at every ale house, and drink when we are dry,
Bb  F   C7   Dm  Am    Gm        Dm
So quickly on the road, my love, we'll marry by and by.


        Dm   C Dm F   Gm          Dm
O Harry, dear Harry, you mind what I do say,
        F   C7  F Bb  F     C7    F C7
My feet they are so tender I cannot march away,
        F   Gm  F Bb    Am    Bb    C
And besides, my dearest Harry, though I'm in love with thee,
BbF    C7    Dm  Am   Gm       Dm
I am not fit for cruel wars in High Germany.


        Dm   C  Dm F   Gm          Dm
O cursed were the cruel wars that ever they should rise,
        F   C7   F Bb F        C7    F C7
And out of merry England press many a lad likewise!
        F   Gm  F Bb    Am    Bb    C
They pressed young Harry from me, likewise my brothers three,
Bb  F    C7   Dm  Am   Gm       Dm
And sent them to the cruel wars in High Germany.
```

SONGS WITH MORE THAN THREE CHORDS IN VARIOUS MAJOR AND MINOR KEYS

Geordie

When the meter changes to $\frac{3}{2}$ just play one more set of four arpeggios, as indicated above the music.

Suggested Strum: Arpeggios

As I walked out - on a Lon - don___ bridge, One mist - y morn - ing ear - ly, I o - ver - heard a fair pret - ty maid was la - ment - ing___ for her Geor - die. ___

Em · · · · D · · · C · · · G
Ah, my Geordie will be hanged in a golden chain
Em · · · · G · · · D
'Tis not the chain of many
Em · · · · G · · · D · · · Bm
He was born of King's royal breed
C · · · G · · · B7 · · · Em
And lost to a virtuous lady.

Em · · · · D · · · C · · · G
Go bridle me my milk white steed
Em · · · · G · · · D
Go bridle me my pony
Em · · · · G · · · D · · · Bm
I will ride to London's court
C · · · G · · · B7 · · · Em
To plead for the life of Geordie.

Em · · · · D · · · C · · · G
Ah my Geordie never stole nor cow nor calf
Em · · · · G · · · D
He never hurted any
Em · · · · G · · · D · · · Bm
Stole sixteen of the King's royal deer
C · · · G · · · B7 · · · Em
And he sold them in Kilkenny.

Em · · · · D · · · C · · · G
Two pretty babies have I born
Em · · · · G · · · D
The third lies in my body
Em · · · · G · · · D · · · Bm
I'd freely part with them everyone
C · · · G · · · B7 · · · Em
If you'd spare the life of Geordie.

Em · · · · D · · · C · · · G
The judge looked over his left shoulder,
Em · · · · G · · · D
He said, "Fair maid, I'm sorry."
Em · · · · G · · · D · · · Bm
Said, "Fair maid, you must be gone
C · · · G · · · B7 · · · Em
For I cannot pardon Geordie."

Em · · · · D · · · C · · · G
Ah, my Geordie will be hanged in a golden chain
Em · · · · G · · · D
'Tis not the chain of many
Em · · · · G · · · D · · · Bm
Stole sixteen of the King's royal deer
C · · · G · · · B7 · · · Em
And he sold them in Kilkenny.

2-21

Other Side Of Jordan

Suggested Strum: Brush Stroke

It rained for-ty days and it rained for-ty nights, and it rained in the Al-le-ghe-ny moun-tains, It rained for-ty hors-es and a Dom-i-neck-er mule and they land-ed on the oth-er side of Jor-dan.

Chorus

Take off your o-ver-coat and roll up your sleeves Jor-dan is a hard road to trav-el Take off your o-ver-coat and roll up your sleeves, Jor-dan is a hard road to trav-el I be-lieve.

C   Em   F C
The public schools and the public fools
Am   D7   G7
Are raising quite an alarm,
C   Em   F   C
Get a country man educated just a little
G7   C
And he ain't going to work on the farm. *Chorus*

C   Em   F   C
I don't know, but I believe I'm right
Am   D7   G7
The auto's ruined the country,
C   Em   F   C
Let's go back to the horse and buggy
G7   C
And try to save some money. *Chorus*

C   Em   F   C
I know a man that's an evangelist,
Am   D7   G7
Tabernacle's always full,
C   Em   F   C
People come for miles around
G7   C
Just to hear him shoot the bull. *Chorus*

C   Em   F   C
You can talk about your evangelists,
Am   D7   G7
You can talk about Mister Ford, too,
C   Em   F   C
But Henry is a-shaking more hell out of folks
G7   C
Than all the evangelists do. *Chorus*

My Mother Chose My Husband

Suggested Strum: Thumb Pluck Arpeggios

My moth-er chose my hus-band, a law-yer's son was he, When on the wed-ding night he came to bed with me.

Chorus
Ah ha ha, that's no way to, Ah ha ha, that can't be.

| G | D7 | G | D7 |
When on the wedding night he came to bed with me,
| G | Em | Am | A7 | D |
He bit me on the shoulder and almost broke my knee. *Chorus*

| G | D7 | G | D7 |
He bit me on the shoulder and almost broke my knee,
| G | Em | Am | A7 | D |
I called my waiting woman, "Come quickly, Marjorie!" *Chorus*

| G | D7 | G | D7 |
I called my waiting woman, "Come quickly, Marjorie!
| G | Em | Am | A7 | D |
Go tell mama I'm dying. Bid her come hastily." *Chorus*

| G | D7 | G | D7 |
"Go tell mama I'm dying. Bid her come hastily."
| G | Em | Am | A7 | D |
Mama came to my bedside before I could count three. *Chorus*

| G | D7 | G | D7 |
Mama came to my bedside before I could count three,
| G | Em | Am A7 | D |
"Cheer up, my girl, what ails you will never kill," said she. *Chorus*

| G | D7 | G | D7 |
"Cheer up, my girl, what ails you will never kill," said she.
| G | Em | Am | A7 | D |
"If I had died of that, child, God knows where you would be." *Chorus*

| G | D7 | G | D7 |
"If I had died of that, child, God knows where you would be.
| G | Em | Am | A7 | D |
"So if you die, my daughter, I'll grave you splendidly." *Chorus*

| G | D7 | G | D7 |
"So if you die, my daughter, I'll grave you splendidly.
| G | Em | Am A7 | D |
"Then carve upon your tombstone, where everyone can see..." *Chorus*

| G | D7 | G | D7 |
"Then carve upon your tombstone, where everyone can see:
| G | Em | Am | A7 D |
'The only girl who couldn't survive that malady.'" *Chorus*

The Young Man Who Wouldn't Hoe Corn

Suggested Strum: Brush Stroke

I'll sing you a song and it's not ver-y long, It's a-bout a young man who would-n't hoe corn, The rea-son why, I can't tell, This young man was al-ways well. _____

G
In September his corn was knee high,
D Em
In October he laid it by,
G   B7   Em
In November there came a great frost
              D   Em
And all this young man's corn was lost.

G
He went to the field and there peeped in,
                        D   Em
The jimpson weeds were up to his chin,
G   B7   Em
The careless weeds they grew so high,
                    D   Em
Enough for to make this young man cry.

G
In the winter I was told
          D   Em
He went courting very bold,
G   B7   Em
When his courtship first begun—
                  D   Em
"My kind sir, did you make any corn?"

G
"No, kind miss," was his reply,
        D   Em
"Long ago I've laid it by,
G   B7   Em
It wasn't worth while to strive in vain,
                D   Em
For I didn't expect to make one grain."

G
"Here you are, a-wantin' me to wed,
                        D   Em
And cannot make your own cornbread!
G   B7   Em
Single I am and single I'll remain
                D   Em
For a lazy man I won't maintain."

G
"Go down yonder to the pretty little widder,
                              D   Em
And I hope, by heck, that you don't git her!"—
G   B7   Em
She gave him the mitten, shore as you're born,
              D   Em
All because he wouldn't hoe corn.

2-24

Cosher Bailey's Engine

Suggested Strum: All Arpeggios

Cosh - er Bail - ey had an en - gine, It was al - ways want - ing mend - ing, And ac - cord - ing to the pow - er, she could do four miles an hour. — Did you ev - er see, did you ev - er see, Did you ev - er see such a fun - ny thing be - fore?

Chorus
Faster
Thumb Pluck
Arpeggios

D
On the night run up from Gower,
Em   **A7**
She did twenty mile an hour,
Bm
As she whistled through the station
A7
Man, she frightened half the nation. *Chorus*

D
Cosher bought her second-hand,
Em   **A7**
And he painted her so grand,
Bm
When the driver went to oil her
A7
Man, she nearly burst her boiler. *Chorus*

D
Cosher Bailey's sister Lena,
Em   **A7**
She was living up in Blaina,
Bm
She could knit and darn our stockings
A7
But her cooking, it was shocking. *Chorus*

D
Cosher Bailey's brother Rupert,
Em   **A7**
He played stand-off-half for Newport,
Bm
When they played against Llanelly,
A7
Someone kicked him in the belly. *Chorus*

D
Cosher Bailey's cousin Julia,
Em   **A7**
She was taken most peculiar,
Bm
Something happened to her liver,
A7
And she overflowed the river. *Chorus*

D
Cosher Bailey's auntie Anna,
Em   **A7**
She played on the grand piano,
Bm
She went, 'ammer, 'ammer, 'ammer,
A7
All the neighbors said, "God damn 'er!" *Chorus*

D
Cosher Bailey had a mistress,
Em   **A7**
Once she come to him in distress.
Bm
When the doctor asked the question,
A7
She said, "Only indigestion." *Chorus*

D
Yes, Cosher Bailey he did die,
Em   **A7**
In the coffin he did lie,
Bm
But, alas, they heard a knocking,
A7
Cosher Bailey, only joking. *Chorus*

The Man On The Flying Trapeze

Suggested Strum: 3/4 Arpeggios

Once I was hap-py, but now I'm for-lorn, Like an old coat that is
Left in this wide world to fret and to

tat-tered and torn. mourn, Be-trayed by a maid in her teens.

— Now this girl that I loved, she was hand-some and fair, And I

tried all I knew her to please.— But I nev-er could please her one

quar-ter so well, As the man on the fly-ing tra-peze. He

flies through the air with the great-est of ease, This dar-ing young
move-ments are grace-ful, All girls does he

man on the fly-ing tra-peze. His please. And my

love he has pur-loined a-way._____

G   E7   A7
Now the young man by name was Señor Boni Slang,

D7   G   Gdim G
Tall, big and handsome, as well made as Chang.

           E7   A7
Where'er he appeared, how the hall loudly rang,

D7   G
With ovations from all people there.

Em   B7
He'd smile from the bar on the people below

Em   B7
And one night he smiled on my love,

           Em
She winked back at him, and she shouted "Bravo!"

B7   Em D7
As he hung by his nose from above.   *Chorus*

2-26

```
G          E7      A7                      G          E7         A7
One night I as usual went to her home,    Some months after that I went into a hall;
D7                    G   GdimG             D7                G    Gdim G
And found there her mother and father alone. To my surprise I found there on the wall
         E7       A7                               E7        A7
I asked for my love, and soon 'twas made known, A bill in red letters which did my heart gall,
D7              G                          D7                 G
To my horror, that she'd run away.        That she was appearing with him.
Em                    B7                   Em                     B7
She packed up her boxes and eloped in the night, He'd taught her gymnastics, and dressed her in tights
Em                 B7                      Em                   B7
With him with the greatest of ease.       To help him to live at great ease.
         Em                                        Em
From two stories high he had lowered her down He'd made her assume a masculine name,
   B7              Em  D7                     B7              Em  D7
To the ground on his flying trapeze.  Chorus And now she goes on the trapeze.  Chorus
```

Final Chorus:

```
         G          E7        A7
She floats through the air with the greatest of ease;
D7                 G    Gdim G
You'd think her a man on the flying trapeze.
         E7       A7
She does all the work while he takes his ease,
D7                         G
And that's what's become of my love.
```

The Good Boy

Suggested Strum: All Arpeggios

```
              D              G            D
I have never cut throats, even when I yearned to.
              A          E7          A
Never sang dirty songs that my fancy turned to;
          B7       Em        A7          D
I have been a nice boy and done what was expected,
          Bm       G          D
I shall be an old bum loved but unrespected.
```

Cold Water

Cold water, cold water for me. There's noth-ing so pure and so free.____ I'll go to the brook and I'll go to the spring, And o-ver the bub-bles I mer-ri-ly sing. Cold wa-ter, cold wa-ter, Cold wa-ter, cold wa-ter for me.____

C   Dm
There's nothing like water to give

G7   C C#dim
The strength that we need for to live.

D   G   D7   G
So give me a glass of that crystal clear stuff,

D7   G   D7   G7
And give me another—it's never enough. *Chorus*

Mrs. Murphy's Chowder

Won't you bring back, won't you bring back Mis - sus Mur - phy's

chow - der, It was tune - ful, ev - 'ry spoon - ful made you yo - del loud - er.

2-28

Won't you bring back, won't you bring
G

back, Mrs. Murphy's chowder,
D7

From each helping you'll be yelping for

a headache powder;
G

And if they had it where we are, you
D7   **G**

might find an Austin car,
D7

In a plate of Mrs. Murphy's chowder. *Chorus*
G   **A7 D7 G**

Won't you bring back, won't you bring
G

back, Mrs. Murphy's chowder,
D7

You can pack it, you can stack it, all

around the larder.
G

The plumber died the other day; they
D7   **G**

embalmed him right away,
D7

In a bowl of Mrs. Murphy's chowder. *Chorus*
G   **A7 D7 G**

Johnny Todd

Suggested Strum: Thumb-finger Pluck

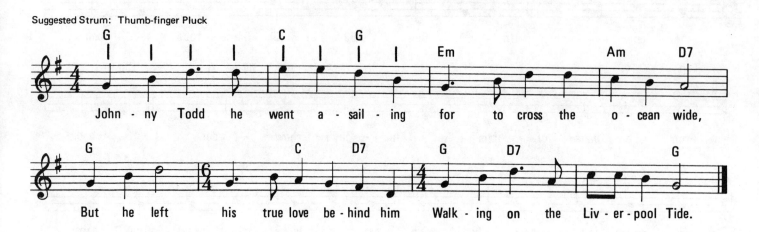

John - ny Todd he went a - sail - ing for to cross the o - cean wide,

But he left his true love be - hind him Walk - ing on the Liv - er - pool Tide.

G	C	G
For a week she wept full sorely,

Em	Am	D7
Tore her hair and wrung her hands,

G	C	D7
Till she met with another sailor

G	D7	G
Walking on the Liverpool sands.

G	C	G
Oh fair maid, why are you weeping

Em	Am	D7
For your Johnny gone to sea?

G	C	D7
If you'll wed with me tomorrow

G	D7	G
I will kind and constant be.

G	C	G
I will buy you sheets and blankets,

Em	Am	D7
I'll buy you a wedding ring;

G	C	D7
You shall have a silver cradle

G	D7	G
For to rock the baby in.

G	C	G
Johnny Todd came home from sailing,

Em	Am	D7
Sailing o'er the ocean wide;

G	C	D7
But he found that his fair and false one

G	D7	G
Was another sailor's bride.

G	C	G
Now young men who go a-sailing,

Em	Am	D7
For to fight the foreign foe;

G	C	D7
Do not leave your love like Johnny,

G	D7	G
Marry her before you go.

The Golden Vanity

Suggested Strum: Brush Stroke

There was a loft-y ship, And she put out to sea, And the
name of the ship was the Gold-en Van-i-ty, As she
sailed up-on the low and lone-some low,
As she sailed up-on the lone-some sea.

C F	C	G7	C		

She had not been out but two weeks or three

C7   F
When she was overtaken by a Turkish Revelee

C
As she sailed upon. . .*Chorus*

C F   C   G7   C
Then up spake our little cabin boy

C7   F
Saying "What will you give me if I will them destroy

C
If I sink them in. . ." *Chorus*

C   F   C   G7   C
"O, the man that them destroys," our captain then replied,

C7   F
"Five thousand pounds and my daughter for his bride

C
If he sinks them in. . ." *Chorus*

C F   C   G7   C
Then the boy smote his breast and down jumped he.

C7   F
He swum until he came to the Turkish Revelee

C
As she sailed upon. . .*Chorus*

C F   C   G7   C
He had a little tool that was made for the use

C7   F
He bored nine holes in her hull all at once

C
And he sunk her in. . .*Chorus*

C F   C   G7   C
He swum back to his ship and he beat upon the side

C7   F
Cried, "Captain, pick me up for I'm wearied with the tide

C
I am sinking in. . ." *Chorus*

C   F   C   G7   C
"No! I will not pick you up" the captain then replied

C7   F
"I will shoot you, I will drown you, I will sink you in the tide,

C
I will sink you in. . ." *Chorus*

C F   C   G7   C
"If it was not for the love that I bear for your men,

C7   F
I would do unto you as I did unto 'them'

C
I would sink you in. . ." *Chorus*

C F   C   G7   C
Then the boy bowed his head and down sunk he

C7   F
Farewell, farewell to the Golden Vanity.

C
As she sails upon. . .*Chorus*

The Housewife's Lament

Suggested Strum: **3/4** Arpeggios

One day I was walk - ing, I heard a com - plain - ing, And saw an old

wom - an, the pic - ture of gloom. She gazed at the mud on her

door - step ('twas rain - ing) And this was her song as she wield - ed her broom.

Chorus

Oh, life is a toil, __ and love is a trou - ble, __ Beau - ty will

fade __ and rich - es will flee. Plea - sures, they dwin - dle and pric - es, they

dou - ble, And noth - ing is as I would wish it to be.

| G | | C | G |
"There's too much of worriment goes to a bonnet,
| D7 | | | G |
There's too much of ironing goes to a shirt.
| | | C | G |
There's nothing that pays for the time you waste on it,
| D7 | | | G |
There's nothing that lasts us but trouble and dirt." *Chorus*

| G | | C | G |
"In March it is mud, it is slush in December,
| D7 | | | G |
The midsummer breezes are loaded with dust.
| | | C | G |
In fall the leaves litter, in muddy September
| D7 | | | G |
The wallpaper rots and the candlesticks rust." *Chorus*

| G | | C | G |
"There are worms on the cherries and slugs on the roses,
| D7 | | | G |
And ants in the sugar and mice in the pies.
| | | C | G |
The rubbish of spiders no mortal supposes,
| D7 | | | G |
And ravaging roaches and damaging flies." *Chorus*

| G | | C | G |
"It's sweeping at six and it's dusting at seven,
| D7 | | | G |
It's victuals at eight and it's dishes at nine.
| | | C | G |
It's potting and panning from ten to eleven,
| D7 | | | G |
We scarce break our fast till we plan how to dine." *Chorus*

2-32

```
         G                              C      G
"With grease and with grime from corner to center,
         D7                        G
Forever at war and forever alert.
                                   C      G
No rest for a day lest the enemy enter,
         D7                              G
I spend my whole life in the struggle with dirt." Chorus
```

```
         G                              C      G
"Last night in my dreams I was stationed forever,
         D7                              G
On a far little rock in the midst of the sea.
                                   C      G
My one chance of life was a ceaseless endeavor,
         D7                              G
To sweep off the waves as they swept over me." Chorus
```

```
         G                              C      G
"Alas! 'Twas no dream—ahead I behold it,
         D7                        G
I see I am helpless my fate to avert."
                              C      G
She lay down her broom, her apron she folded,
         D7                        G
She lay down and died and was buried in dirt. Chorus
```

The Hayseed

Suggested Strum: **3/4** Arpeggios

```
        C                    Am
He went to a hotel, he engaged him a room;
G7               C
It cost him five dollars a minit.
         Em   Am   C
But he did not care, he had money to spare;
G7                          C
This hayseed was bound to be in it.
```

```
        C                    Am
He went to his room, he blew out the gas,
G7               C
He pulled down the bed and got in it.
         Em   Am   C
Next morning at nine, in a coffin of pine
G7                          C
This hayseed was strictly dead in it.
```

We'll Rant And We'll Roar

Suggested Strum: **3/4** Arpeggios

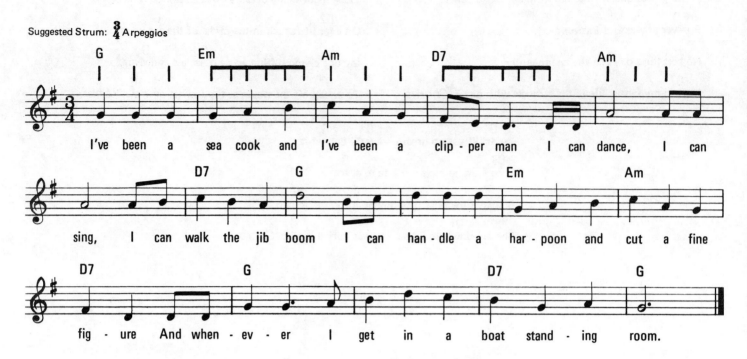

I've been a sea cook and I've been a clip-per man I can dance, I can sing, I can walk the jib boom I can han-dle a har-poon and cut a fine fig-ure And when-ev-er I get in a boat stand-ing room.

Chorus:

       G   Em   Am   D7
We'll rant and we'll roar like true born young whalermen,

     Am   D7   G
We'll rant and we'll roar on deck and below,

             Em   Am   D7
Until we strike Gay Head on old Martha's Vineyard,

        G   D7   G
And straight up the channel to New Bedford we'll go. *Chorus*

      G   Em   Am   D7
I went to a dance one night in old Tumbez,

     Am   D7   G
There were lots of fine girls there as nice as you'd wish,

           Em   Am   D7
There was one pretty maiden a-chewin tobacco,

     G   D7   G
Just like a young kitten, a-chewin' fresh fish. *Chorus*

      G   Em   Am   D7
I was in Turkeywanna last year on a whaler,

   Am   D7   G
I bought some fine gifts for the girls on the Bay;

           Em   Am   D7
And I bought me a pipe—they called it a "Meerschaum,"

    G   D7   G
But it melted like butter, all on a hot day. *Chorus*

       G   Em   Am   D7
Here's a health to the girls of old Turkeywanna,

     Am   D7   G
Here's a health to the girls of far off Malee.

         Em   Am   D7
And let you be jolly, don't be melancholy,

     G   D7   G
I could marry yez all, but my wife won't agree. *Chorus*

Deep Blue Sea

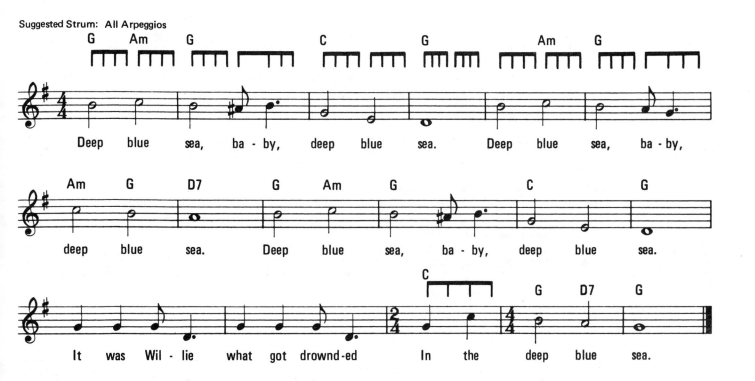

Suggested Strum: All Arpeggios

Deep blue sea, ba-by, deep blue sea. Deep blue sea, ba-by,

deep blue sea. Deep blue sea, ba-by, deep blue sea.

It was Wil-lie what got drownd-ed In the deep blue sea.

G Am G   C   G
Dig his grave with a silver spade.

   Am G   Am G D7
Dig his grave with a silver spade.

G Am G   C   G
Dig his grave with a silver spade.

It was Willie what got drownded

C   G   D7 G
In the deep blue sea.

    G Am G   C   G
Golden sun bring him back again.

     Am G   Am G D7
Golden sun bring him back again.

    G Am G   C   G
Golden sun bring him back again.

    It was Willie what got drownded

    C   G   D7 G
    In the deep blue sea.

Repeat verse one

G Am G   C   G
Lower him down with a golden chain.

   Am G   Am G D7
Lower him down with a golden chain.

G Am G   C   G
Lower him down with a golden chain.

It was Willie what got drownded

C   G   D7 G
In the deep blue sea.

The Ship That Never Returned

Suggested Strum: Thumb Pluck Árpeggios

On a sum - mer's day while the waves were rip - pling, with a
sweet fare - wells, there were lov - ing sig - nals, While a

qui - et and a gen - tle breeze;___ A___ ship set sail with a
form was yet dis - cerned;___ Though they knew it not, 'twas a

car - go lad - en for a post be - yond the sea. There were
sol - emn part - ing, For the ship, she nev'r re - turned.

Chorus

Did she ev - er re - turn? No, she nev - er re - turned, and her

fate is still un - learned,___ Though for years and years the

fond ones wait - ed, For the ship that nev - er re - turned.___

C   F
Said a feeble lad to his anxious mother,
C   D7   G G7
"I must cross the wide, wide sea;
C   F
For they say, perchance, in a foreign climate,
C   G7   C
There is health and strength for me."
F
'Twas a gleam of hope in a maze of danger,
C   D7   G G7
And her heart for her youngest yearned;
C   F
Yet she sent him forth with a smile and blessing
C   G7   C
On the ship that never returned. *Chorus*

C   F
"Only one more trip," said a gallant seaman,
C   D7   G G7
As he kissed his weeping wife;
C   F
"Only one more bag of the golden treasure,
C   G7   C
And 'twill last us all through life.
F
Then I'll spend my days in my cozy cottage,
C   D7   G G7
And enjoy the rest I've earned;"
C   F
But alas! poor man! for he sailed commander
C   G7   C
Of the ship that never returned. *Chorus*

The Blue-Tail Fly

Brush down on 1st beat of each measure or chord change

And when he'd ride in the afternoon,
I'd follow after with a hickory broom;
The pony being like to shy
When bitten by a blue-tail fly. *Chorus*

One day he ride around the farm,
The flies so numerous, they did swarm.
One chanced to bite him on the thigh;
The devil take the blue-tail fly! *Chorus*

The pony run, he jump, he pitch;
He threw my master in the ditch.
He died—and the jury wondered why—
The verdict was the blue-tail fly. *Chorus*

They laid him under a 'simmon tree;
His epitaph is there to see:
"Beneath this stone I'm forced to lie,
A victim of the blue-tail fly." *Chorus*

Beans, Bacon and Gravy

Suggested Strum: Thumb Pluck Arpeggios

I was born long a-go in eigh-teen nine-ty-four, And I've
hun-gry, I've been cold, and now I'm grow-ing old, But the
wake up in the morn-ing and an-oth-er day is dawn-ing I

seen man-y a pan-ic, I will own. I've been
worst I've seen is nine-teen thir-ty
know I'll have an-oth-er mess of

one. Oh, those beans, ba-con and gra-vy, they
beans.

al-most drive me cra-zy, I eat them till I see them in my dreams. When I

G
We congregate each morning,
C   G
At the country barn at dawning,
A7 D7
And everyone is happy so it seems,
G
But when our work is done,
C   G
We file in one by one,
D7   G
And thank the Lord for one more mess of beans. *Chorus*

G
We have Hooverized on butter;
C   G
For milk we've only water,
A7 D7
And I haven't seen a steak in many a day;
G
As for pies and cakes and jellies,
C   G
We substitute sow-bellies,
D7   G
For which we work the county road each day. *Chorus*

G
If there ever comes a time
C   G
When I have more than a dime,
A7 D7
They will have to put me under lock and key,
G
For I've been broke so long
C   G
I can only sing this song,
D7   G
Of the workers and their misery. *Chorus*

2-38

The Wreck Of The Old Ninety-Seven

Suggested Strum: Thumb Pluck Arpeggios

Well, they gave him his or-ders at Mon-roe, Vir-gin-ia, Say-in'

"Steve, you are way be-hind time. This is not "thir-ty-eight," But it's

old "nine-ty-sev-en." You must put her in-to Dan-ville on time."

```
       A                   D
He turned and said to his black greasy fireman,
       A        B7        E7
"Just shovel on a little more coal,
       A                   D
And when we cross the White Oak Mountain
       A        E7         A
You can watch old 'ninety-seven' roll."


          A                        D
It's a mighty rough road from Lynchburg to Danville,
       A        B7        E7
On a line on a three mile grade,
          A                   D
It was on this grade that he lost his average,
       A        E7    A
You can see what a jump he made.


           A                           D
He was going down the grade makin' ninety miles an hour,
       A        B7         E7
When his whistle broke into a scream,
       A                      D
They found him in the wreck with his hand on the throttle,
       A        E7          A
He was scalded to death by the steam.


        A                  D
Now, ladies, you must all take warning,
       A        B7    E7
From this time now on learn,
       A                           D
Never speak harsh words to your true loving husband,
       A        E7    A
He may leave you and never return.
```

Mighty Day

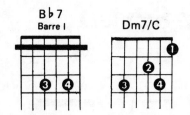

Suggested Strum: Thumb Pluck Arpeggios

I re-mem-ber one Sep-tem-ber, Storm winds swept the

town; Wom-en and chil-dren were dy-in', God!__ Death was all a-

round. Was-n't it a might-y day!_____ Was-n't it a

might-y day!_____ Was-n't it a might-y day, Great

God, that morn-ing when the storm winds swept the town!

Dm	A7
There was a seawall there in Galveston,	
Dm	A7
To keep the waters down;	
Dm	Gm
But the high tide from the ocean, God,	
A7	Dm
Put water into the town. *Chorus*	

Dm	A7
Well, the trumpets gave them warning,	
Dm	A7
You'd better leave this place;	
Dm	Gm
But they never meant to leave their homes	
A7	Dm
Till death was in their face. *Chorus*	

Dm	A7
The waters, like some river,	
Dm	A7
Came rushing to and fro;	
Dm	Gm
Seen my father drowning, God,	
A7	Dm
I watched my mother go. *Chorus*	

Dm	A7
The sea began to rollin ,	
Dm	A7
The ships they could not land,	
Dm	Gm
Heard a captain crying, "God,	
A7	Dm
Please save this drowning man!" *Chorus*	

The Ox-Driving Song

Suggested Strum: Brush Stroke

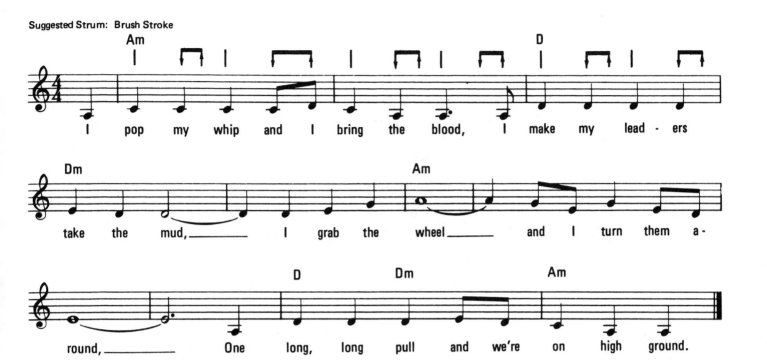

I pop my whip and I bring the blood, I make my lead-ers take the mud,_____ I grab the wheel_____ and I turn them a-round,_____ One long, long pull and we're on high ground.

Chorus:

Am
To my roll, to my roll, to my ride-e-o,

D   Dm
To my roll, to my roll, to my ride-e-o,

Am
To my ride-e-o, to my ru-de-o,

D   Dm   Am
To my roll, to my roll, to my ride-e-o.

Am
On the fourteenth day of October-o,

D   Dm
I hitched my team in order-o.

Am
To drive to the hills of Saludio.

D   Dm   Am
To my roll, to my roll, to my ride-e-o. *Chorus*

Am
When I got there the hills were steep,

D   Dm
A tender-hearted person'd weep

Am
To hear me cuss and pop my whip,

D   Dm Am
To see my oxen pull and slip. *Chorus*

Am
When I get home I'll have revenge,

D   Dm
I'll land my family among my friends.

Am
I'll bid adieu to the whip and line,

D   Dm   Am
And drive no more in the wintertime. *Chorus*

As I Roved Out

Suggested Strum: All Arpeggios

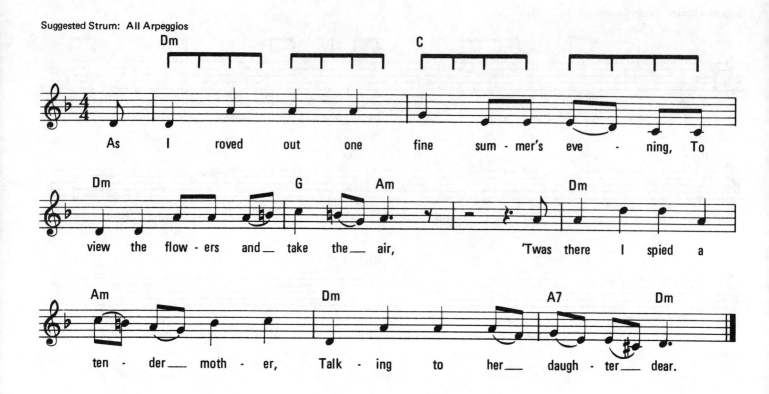

As I roved out one fine sum-mer's eve-ning, To view the flow-ers and take the air, 'Twas there I spied a ten-der mother, Talk-ing to her daugh-ter dear.

      Dm   C
Saying,"Daughter, O daughter, I'll have you to marry,

  Dm   G   Am
No longer to lead a sweet single life."

    Dm   Am
"O mother, O mother, I'd rather tarry

  Dm   A7   Dm
To be some brave young sailor's wife."

    Dm   C
"O a sailor boy likes all for to wander,

  Dm   G   Am
He will prove your overthrow.

  Dm   Am
O daughter, you are better to wed with a farmer,

  Dm   A7   Dm
For to the seas he ne'er do go."

     Dm   C
"O mother, I cannot wed with a farmer,

    Dm   G   Am
Though he decks me with diamonds bright,

    Dm   Am
I'll wait for my love with the tarry, tarry trousers,

    Dm   A7   Dm
For he's my darling and my heart's delight."

The River In The Pines

Suggested Strum: All Arpeggios ($\frac{3}{4}$)

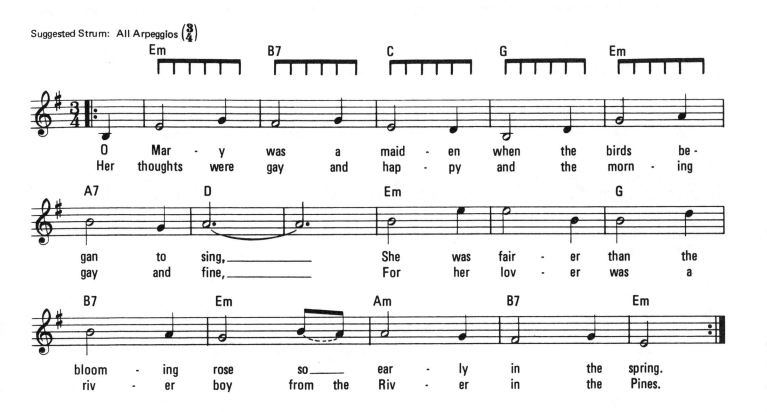

O Mar - y was a maid - en when the birds be -
Her thoughts were gay and hap - py and the morn - ing

gan to sing, _____ She was fair - er than the
gay and fine, _____ For her lov - er was a

bloom - ing rose so_____ ear - ly in the spring.
riv - er boy from the Riv - er in the Pines.

     Em B7   C   G   Em A7   D
Now Charlie he got married to his Mary in the spring,

Em   G B7 Em Am B7 Em
When the trees were budding early and the birds began to sing.

      B7 C   G   Em A7   D
"But early in the autumn when the fruit is on the vine,

Em   G B7   Em Am B7 Em
I'll return to you, my darling, from the River in the Pines."

     Em B7   C G Em   A7   D
'Twas early in the morning in Wisconsin's dreary clime,

Em   G B7 Em Am B7 Em
When he rode the fatal rapids for that last and fatal time.

      B7 C G   Em   A7   D
They found his body lying on the rocky shore below

Em   G B7 Em Am   B7   Em
Where the silent water ripples and the whispering cedars blow.

     Em B7   C G   Em   A7   D
Now every raft of lumber that comes down the Chippeway,

  Em   G   B7 Em Am B7   Em
There's a lonely grave that's visited by the drivers on their way.

       B7   C G Em   A7   D
They plant wild flowers upon it in the morning fair and fine,

Em   G   B7 Em Am B7   Em
'Tis the grave of two young lovers from the River in the Pines.

Beautiful Dreamer

Suggested Strum: All Arpeggios (**3/4**)

by STEPHEN FOSTER

Beau - ti - ful dream - er, wake un - to me,____
Sounds of the rude world heard in the day,____
Gone are the cares of life's bus - y throng,____

Star - light and dew - drops are wait - ing for thee.____
Lulled by the moon - light have all passed a -
Beau - ti - ful dream - er a - wake un - to *To Coda*

way.____ Beau - ti - ful dream - er, queen of my song,____

D. C. al Coda

List while I woo thee with soft mel - o - dy.____

Coda

me.____ Beau - ti - ful dream - er, a - wake un - to me.____

C   Dm
Beautiful dreamer, out on the sea
G7   C
Mermaids are chanting the wild Lorelei,
            Dm
Over the streamlet vapors are borne
G7   C
Waiting to fade at the bright coming morn.
G7   C
Beautiful dreamer, beam on my heart
Am   D7   G7
E'en as the morn on the streamlet and sea,
C   Dm
Then will all clouds of sorrow depart.
G7   C E7 Am
Beautiful dreamer, awake unto me.
          F   C   G7   C
Beautiful dreamer, awake unto me.

Blow Away The Morning Dew

Suggested Strum: Thumb Pluck Arpeggios

	G	Em	
	He looked high, he looked low,		
	C D7 G		
	He cast an under look;		
	Em Am		
	And there he saw a fair pretty maid,		
	Em D C G Am		
	Beside the watery brook. *Chorus*		

G   Em
He looked high, he looked low,
C   D7   G
He cast an under look;
   Em   Am
And there he saw a fair pretty maid,
Em D C G   Am
Beside the watery brook. *Chorus*

G   Em
Cast over me my mantle fair
C   D7   G
And pin it o'er my gown;
   Em   Am
And if you will, take hold my hand,
Em D C G   Am
And I will be your own. *Chorus*

G   Em
If you come down to my father's house,
C   D7   G
Which is walled all around,
   Em   Am
Then you shall have my maidenhead
Em D C G   Am
And twenty thousand pound. *Chorus*

G   Em
He mounted on a milk-white steed,
C   D7   G
And she upon another;
   Em   Am
And then they rode upon the lane
Em D C G   Am
Like sister and like brother. *Chorus*

G   Em
As they were riding on alone,
C   D7   G
They saw some pooks of hay.
   Em   Am
Oh, is this not a pretty place
Em D C G   Am
For girls and boys to play? *Chorus*

G   Em
But when they came to her father's gate,
C   D7   G
So nimble she popped in,
   Em   Am
And said: "There is a fool without,
Em D C G   Am
And here's a maid within." *Chorus*

G   Em
And if you meet a lady gay
C   D7   G
As you go by the hill,
   Em   Am
And if you will not when you may,
Em D C G   Am
You shall not when you will. *Chorus*

Basic Guitar Chords

The following symbols are used in this chart.

P = Primary Bass String   O = Open string to be played
A = Alternate Bass String   X = String not to be played
━━ = Barre - 1st finger covers all six strings.

The number to the right of some of the diagrams indicates the fret.
Some of the fingerings presented here may differ from the way they appeared in the text. Both are correct.

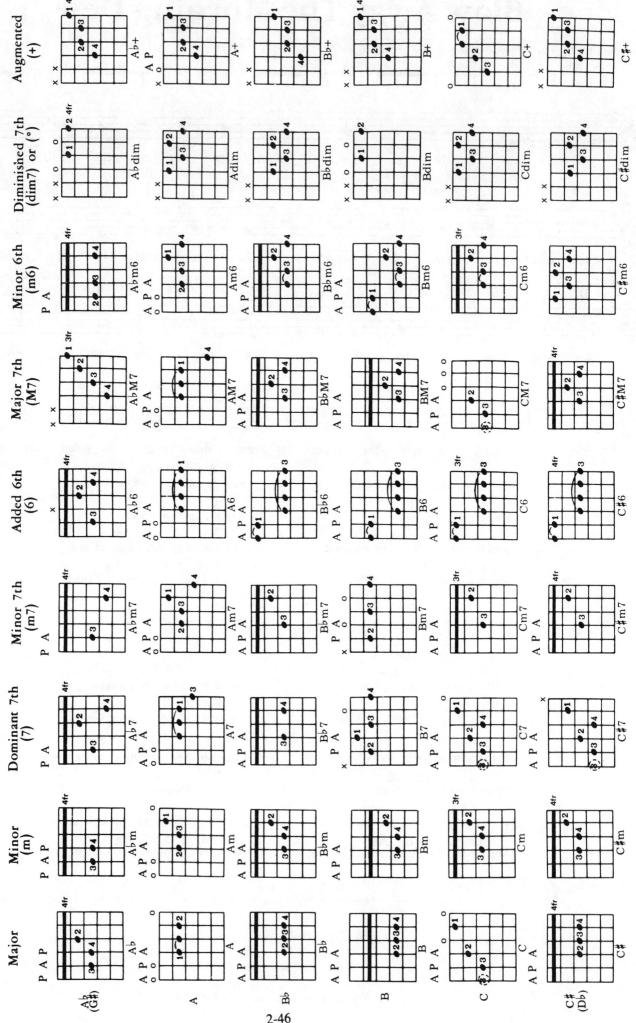

2-46

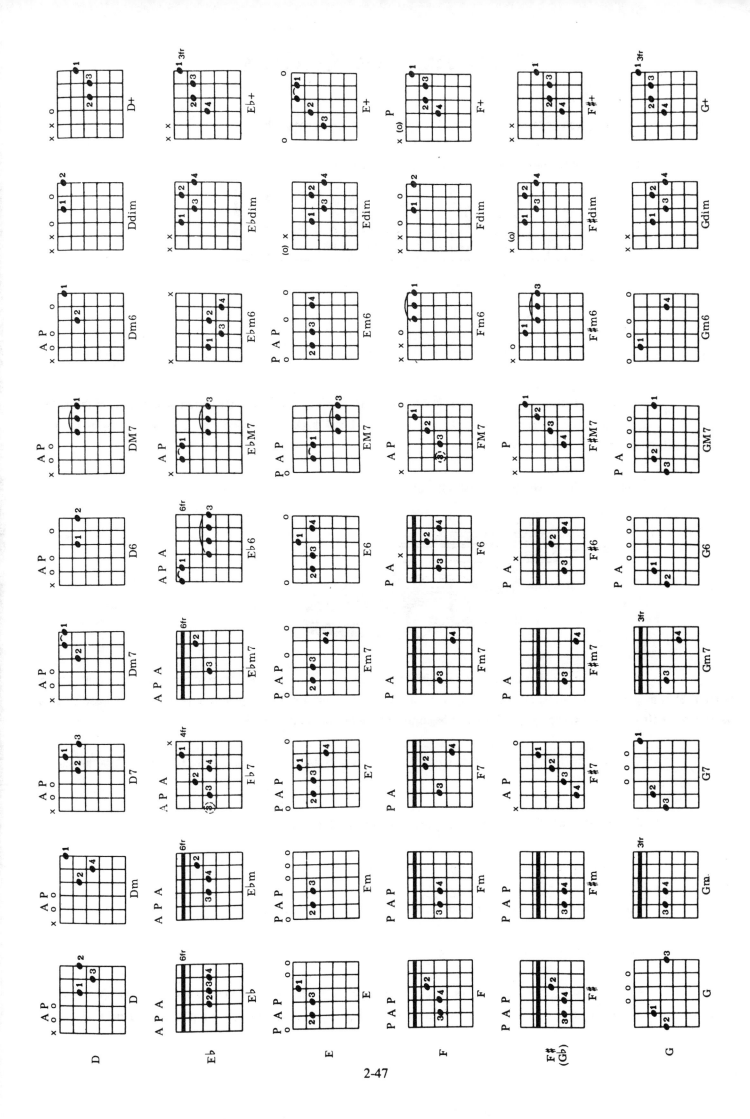

Tuning The Guitar

Tightening a string raises the pitch and loosening a string lowers the pitch.

The strings of the guitar relate to notes of a piano as follows:

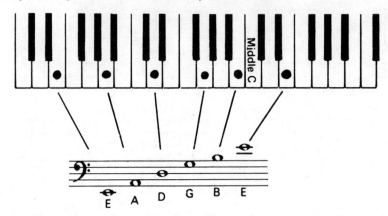

If you have a piano strike the proper key and listen to how it compares with the corresponding string of the guitar. Make whatever adjustment in the guitar string your ear tells you to do. Check back to the piano again and listen to the guitar once more. Does it sound right?. . .Go on to the next string.

A guitar pitch pipe will give you the notes of each string.

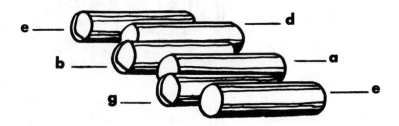

If no standard pitch is available with which to compare your guitar you must learn to tune your instrument relative to itself. Start by playing the sixth string and judging if it "seems to sound and feel" reasonably in tune. This is a necessarily vague statement but after some experience you will actually begin to develop this mysterious sense.

Then play the fifth fret of the sixth string. This gives us A. 1t should be the same as the fifth string. After tuning the A string to this note—

Play the fifth fret of the A string. That gives us D. Tune the D string.

Play the fifth fret of the fourth string. This gives us G. Tune the G string.

Play the *fourth* fret of the third string. This gives us B. Tune the B string.

Play the fifth fret of the B string. This gives us E. Tune the E string.

Compare the sixth and first strings. They should both sound "like E," two octaves apart. Play an E minor chord slowly—note by note. If something sounds off adjust that string. In the beginning it's trial and error. Keep at it. Good luck!